THE CONTRACT WITH AMERICA

VERSUS

THE COVENANT WITH GOD

THE CONTRACT WITH AMERICA

VERSUS

THE COVENANT WITH GOD

By
Reverend Dr. William M. James
Executive Director, Ministerial
Interfaith Association

ISBN: 0-75960-649-8

This book is printed on acid free paper.

1stBooks – rev. 2/9/01

TABLE OF CONTENTS

FOREWORD
By
David H. Dinkins
106th Mayor, City of New York

The Reverend Dr. James, by reflecting on the roots of public social policy, causes us to reexamine the central issue of the extent to which American urban society cares for the "least of us." He ably makes the point that the seminal document that has guided national and local public policy since the 1994 elections, termed the "Contract with America," has been at tremendous odds with the higher principle upon which this nation was founded – what he describes by way of contrast as the "Covenant with God." Dr. James's analysis places these developments in the context of this covenant, and he brings to this discussion a rich personal experience, having devoted his entire professional life to serving the spiritual and socioeconomic needs of the people of New York City's communities.

America today is so affluent, and many of its citizens are enjoying a level of personal material comfort unlike that ever before experienced. But, in the absence of a public policy that recognizes the entitlements of all Americans to a share of that comfort, by virtue of our citizenship, a "contract" that relies so heavily on individual largesse does nothing more than pay lip service to those ideals upon which the nation was founded. The so-called "Contract with America" has represented, not an opportunity to exercise greater responsibility to the public good (as it has been touted), but an abdication of that responsibility.

The economies of this country, and of our urban centers, are booming on many levels, but too few are sharing in that bounty. We must, as Dr. James suggests, question, challenge, and act on the fact that conditions are worsening for the poor while the rich continue to live better existences. Lack of access to education, affordable health care, and job opportunities – all these problems – are walking with us into a new century.

As a direct consequence of the Congressional abdication of those principles that endorsed the "inalienable rights" of all Americans, we find ourselves as a nation walking *backwards* into the new century. The "Contractors", as Dr. James refers to the engineers of this political concept, have succeeded in chipping away at too many hard-fought victories that only barely began to address the centuries of injustice suffered by so many Americans…for so long.

Dr. James minces no words in attacking the core beliefs that form the basis of the "Contract", and lays bare the fact that its limited successes have been more a reflection of the will of a minority of special interests than the intent of the majority of a complacent voting public. In this pointed commentary, Dr. James suggests that "the number not voting says more about our troubled nation than the ones who voted for the so-called "Contract." And, as Dr. Martin Luther King, Jr. cautioned us, and as the Reverend Dr. James reinforces: "When the world looks back on the twentieth century, they will weep not for the atrocities that took place, but for the silence of the good people."

There are those who believe that there may not be a solution. They point out that America's tremendous experiment in peaceful diversity has never been undertaken anywhere else in the world, and that perhaps we should think ourselves fortunate that we as a nation are not plagued by problems and violence as intense as in other areas of the globe.

Yet many of us do believe that there must…and will be a solution. Dr. James suggests that part of the solution lies in recasting the debate about race and class in America in terms of the promise of "life, liberty, and the pursuit of happiness" – a "Covenant with God" as reflected in this nation's founding documents, and not in a "social contract" that denies that promise. The solution also relies on the commitment of people of good will and determination. Such a person is the Reverent William James, and we thank him for this work of devotion.

# # #

INTRODUCTION

The germination of this writing springs from the seed of my experience in my work in the Bronx and Harlem over fifty (50) years. During this time I have had various kinds of contacts with both the world of the Church and the world of Body Politic. At times, it has been difficult to tell one from the other, but the factor for me, has been a distinct line of demarcation, has been the Covenant with God which has come down to us through the faith of Abraham; the courage and clarification of some of the prophets; and the climatic Revelation of God to us through the person of Jesus, the one I believe is the Christ.

Therefore, when I use the phrase "Contract with America" in quoting from and in reference to the book of that title, which was the guideline of the so-called conservatives of the Congress of '94 and '95, I am not limiting this writing to them. The book "Contract with America" is just one stage, or marker, on the highway toward the destiny which some of the so-called "conservatives" and the "Religious Right" would lead us into the future. My contention here is that these ideas of both their book and philosophy are not futuristic at all, but they would turn back the clock to the time when the United States of America was an agrarian society and sparsely populated; to a time when the "industrial revolution" was just taking shape and the conflict concerning slavery was the main social topic. This is not the formula for living in a highly industrial society. One in which Urbanism is geared to be the hub which radiates to all by instant communication. Also a time in which the Industrial Revolution is giving way to a form of "Scientistic (my word) Production" in which "Electronic Automation" is the chief ingredient and the Computer is "Robot King."

In light of this, what we are saying is that old agrarian bucolic styles of handling the poor by the charitable individual acts from the hearts and hands of those who would help, which was a part of an agrarian society, must give way to a more updated way of caring for and handling the uplifting of the poor, aiding children and others in need. Our new method, which is already in progress, must be a part of our social structure. This should no longer depend on a "hit-or-miss" type of aid to those who are in need, but to have a built-in structure which considers this as an obligation for us all.

In thinking of my work in New York and the struggle with the "have nots," has made me sensitive to the past efforts made to alleviate poverty by helping them out of their state of being. This, because I have been part of so many movements of this kind – movements of help and self-help.

My first effort was to serve over a nursery school in Harlem in the early forties – from which I have seen numbers of great persons develop. One of my first wider efforts was to serve with the late Fiorello LaGuardia's "Commission on War Time Care of Children" After this, I became President of one of the Branches of the N.A.A.C.P.; the Vice Chairman of the Board of HARYOU-Act; one of the Founders of the Ministerial Interfaith Association; Board Member of the Opportunity Industrialization Center of New York; Projector of the idea that brought about the Ethnic Minority Local Church Initiative of the United Methodist Church; and the Chairman of the Board and one of the Founders of the Harlem Urban Development Corporation (HUDC). This work and involvement has given me opportunities to see how programs, which have been down-played and ridiculed by many in our present time, have been in reality, the saviors of our present society and have given us hope for the future.

Therefore, it is incumbent upon me to tell our people of the good which has gone before, and to warn them of the dangers ahead if we fail to build on these progressive foundations which have been handed down to the present generation.

I have done this writing as a positive warning to the United States of America and the other Americas. I have done it in the names of the great "liberals" and "progressives" who have given of themselves in thought, hard work, suffering and sacrifice for the aggressive progress, hopes and freedoms which we now enjoy. These are the fruits of their labor to be eaten by us, but the seeds should be passed down to committing generations. I have received so much from them. I cannot continue to enjoy the fruits without seeing it as a legacy to be passed on. Also, I bow my head to God, who through his covenant, gave us the Christ to open the highway to freedom and admonish us to keep the road open so that all of his people can walk thereon.

William James

THE CONTRACT WITH AMERICA

VERSUS

THE COVENANT WITH GOD

The Contract with America seems to be a political gimmick put together in a time of general misgivings about our national, state, and local governments. Some of these are reasonably founded but most are election propaganda and carried out on the idea that this propaganda brought about the election of the "Conservative Right" in the 1994 elections. Some may say that the "Contract" is based on what America wants. This is said in face of the facts that twenty million plus people voted for the Republican Party candidates, out of some two hundred million persons in this nation with over one hundred million eligible to vote. The number not voting says more about our troubled nation than the ones who voted for the "Right Wing." When people are voting for personal "tax cutting" promises it does not necessarily mean that they are voting for the "Contract" that promised individual voters they will pay little tax or no taxes. Many will support politicians for this reason. Further, they are told that they are paying high taxes because of "welfare" programs to help the poor. The code is that the poor are mostly Blacks and Hispanics living off of the middle class Whites (who vote en masse) because the poor are too lazy and shiftless to work and care for themselves and their families. Further, it is said of "Welfare" that the "Aid to Dependent Children" goes, in large part, to teenage mothers who have more children in order to get larger checks.

1

These are generalizations, but when we get down to the recorded statements of "The Contract," the generalizations do not improve. They are propelled into a projection of public policy and further attempts are made to set some of them in concrete in our Constitution.

First, let us start with the title "Contract with America." The word "America," in the context used here, means the United States of America or the Americas. I think the loose use of the word "America" when we mean only a part of America (the U.S.A.) shows forth part of our "Big Brother" complex at best and our domineering arrogance at worse. There are many peoples of the Americas. And what we are attempting to show in this essay is that "The Contract" will have a much wider impact on the whole of the Western Hemisphere than we are willing to admit. The risk of dividing ourselves from the rest of the world means isolationism, which is impossible in the world of the twentieth century, and will increase to a dangerous projection for the twenty-first century of the third millennium.

In its beginning, the document states that "Nothing written before or after the election better defines the difference between the two parties than the document you have in your hands."[1] When one reads the document one does not find this as clear a distinction as one would expect by this statement. History will show that the parties have shifted their positions from time to time and we find one acting like the other at one age and changing through history. The Republicans, who started off as a Party for freedom of Black people in this nation, led the fight for the 13th, 14th and 15th Amendments, the most liberal parts of

---

[1]

the Bill of Rights of the Constitutions, if we include the 18th Amendment which gave women a right to vote. These were the Equal Rights Amendments. They were developed for the correction of grave discrimination toward the Black slaves in some states and all races, colors and genders.

In later history it was the Democratic Party, mostly of the southern states, that formed a solid flank to nullify these Amendments, with the exception of the 18th. The Democrats did accomplish this by denying Blacks the right to vote in the Democratic primary, which was basic in the elections in the south and is fundamental for freedom in a representative democracy. They also denied Blacks the right to equal education, by not providing public schools and equal access to teacher education on or near the level of Whites; Blacks were also denied access to the Courts in any equal way (no jury, no judges, no attorneys). In this way they fostered slavery and afterwards cried "States Rights!"—code words to hide behind the scenes of the persecution of the slaves and former slaves. The states had the rights to allow lynching with no expectation that the lynchers would be brought to justice. They kept the code of Roger Taney, United States Justice of the Supreme Court from 1836-64, who said the "Black man had no right that a White man was bound to honor"[2] The Republicans acquiesced to this treatment of the Black people of this country from the 1880's through 1932. The Franklin Delano Roosevelt administration began to recapture the meaning of this freedom and through Henry Wallace, Harold Ickes Jr. and Roosevelt's wife, Eleanor Roosevelt, began to maneuver for a loosening of the shackles on the Black people.

2

When the Contract with America lays down "individuality" as one of its foundation pillars, this is not new in the rhetoric and not a meaningful commitment. It was said much better in the Declaration of Independence by Thomas Jefferson when he wrote, "We hold these truths to be self evident (or axiomatically perceived) that all men (persons) are created equal and endowed by their <u>Creator</u> with certain <u>inalienable</u> rights (rights inseparable from his/her being). Among these are life, liberty and the pursuit of happiness." To deal with these rights there has to be something deeper and far more substantial than "The Contract with America," a political concept with temporal standing and of short duration. There must be a deeper covenant with God dealing with the true worth of human beings which flows from the Eternal or Metaphysical, to be incorporated into the affairs of human beings in human society. This is what Jefferson meant about the rights of human beings and from whence they came or flowed. They flowed from the live idea that human beings were created by God and did not live at the whims and fancy of a social contract.

The Covenant with God which was transmitted first through Abraham is stated thus, "Now the Lord said to Abraham, Go from your country and your kindred and your father's house to the land that I will show you. And I will make you a nation, and I will bless you and make your name great so that <u>you will be a blessing</u>. I will bless those who bless you, and him who curses you I will curse; <u>and</u> by you <u>all</u> the <u>families</u> of the earth will bless <u>themselves</u>." (Genesis 12:1-4) This is basic and we can see that it is different from the Contract with America; it is as Universal in its scope as the Declaration of Independence has all in mind—the poor, the helpless, the wrongdoers, and the rest.

This Covenant comes to us through Jesus the Christ who laid the dictum that all persons were children of God.

Just as the Contract with America is trying to do with a limited social contract, there has to be a way to put this Covenant together in a working form in order that it will be part of the whole society. However, we must always remember that the idea comes from the concept that there is something or indeed Someone who sets the value standards for human beings; Someone who is outside of the society and will not yield His Covenant to a "social contract" made among human beings and designed to exclude many of His created human beings.

The symbolism of the first 100 days of the "Contract with America" projects a program which comes from and is contrasted with the first 99 days of the Roosevelt administration. Roosevelt took office March 4, 1933 amidst the greatest peace time crisis the nation has ever known. He had campaigned on the theme of "the forgotten man," the working class and the lower underclass that had multiplied because of the wealth which had been piled up by the few. Unemployment was at a new high. There had to be a series of acts to restore morale. To do this he was given unprecedented power by Congress. He projected to the legislative branch of government, in rapid-fire succession, measures which have helped to stabilize the nation since that time. Bank failures were in large numbers and were stabilized by their closings. When they were reopened they were insured up to a certain amount by the Federal government. Roosevelt inaugurated the Civilian Conservation Corp. began a program of public works, and a form of home relief law. The Tennessee Valley Authority was developed and reformed the economics of much of the southeast. He also established the Civil Service Merit

System, the Social Security Act and many more. All of these reached out to the people and shared the national wealth with the people in order that government would not collapse.

The "Contract with America" is admonishing Congress to cut taxes and balance the budget by savings in cutting educational funds, food stamps, other monies for poor families and children. They are doing this in a time of unprecedented prosperity; when stock market dividends have skyrocketed, up more than any time in our history. This is to be contrasted with the gap between the poor and wealthy widening almost daily and both groups growing in number. Homelessness is higher per capita than in the Depression. The "Contract" is going in the opposite direction in much of the document. The "Contract with America" seems to go against the very grain of individual liberty. Many of its sections are far from the idea of freedom that is the keystone of the Roosevelt administration. Roosevelt helped in people's attempt to make freedom or the "pursuit of happiness" a reality in society. Nowhere is this difference more pronounced than in Roosevelt's interpretation of the four freedoms: freedom of worship, freedom of speech, freedom from want and freedom from fear.

Let us start with freedom of speech. This is to give the individual or like-minded groups the right to be heard and to get their points of view over to the public in a fair and honesty way. In this technical world of the last of the twentieth century and the beginning of the twenty-first century, saying something in a civic way means nothing unless one has a conduit through which the public can hear what is being said. Much of the media that spread propaganda daily are closed to the poor and less affluent, while the monied people have access to say what is on their mind. The supreme example of this is in "standing" or running for public office. It does not matter how good one is and what great ideas he/she espouses; there will be no election of them unless money is raised to have access to the media. We hear of a senate race costing seven or eight million dollars and the House of Representative race costing from two hundred thousand to upwards of one million dollars. Freedom of speech is not free if one is going to get over to the public. Contrast this with, let's say, the Lincoln-Douglas debates of 1858, which set pretty clear the issue of a free nation and a slave nation, and would not have a chance today. Lincoln, a man of very modest means, would not have been in the "running" for anything. The days of Trafalgar Square, London, Coopers Union, New York, 7th Avenue and 125 Street, Harlem – where people gathered to discuss in public forums – have gone the way of the democratic forums of Athens and ancient Rome. They have gone without a new method of communicating great ideas for the general public. Most of what we hear is propaganda. Even what little access that is there is destined to be severely cut or eliminated if the "Contract with America" stands. Look what is in the budget cuts: Public Broadcasting, the National Endowment for the Arts and some preferential treatment to access the airways by minority groups. These are the last media left for the public access.

Therefore, when the boast is made by those who wrote the "Contract" that this is a mandate from the people of America one can only see the danger for this great nation. The per capita voting strength in this nation is declining. There were only forty percent plus of the eligible voters who votes for the Republican ticket which was elected.

This does not show a mandate but it does show a grave danger. We should be disturbed by so few people voting. One obvious or most discernible reason is: the propaganda against "big government" has had its effect. Everybody curses "Washington" and those who make it spend millions to get there. The slogan "Give the government back to the people" is an empty cliché. In a representative democracy the people already have back local, state and national government in their hands if they will really elect people who will be their surrogates instead of attempting to be their potentates. To have a representative democracy the electorate must be well informed, thinking for the best for the whole and from this aiming at well-being for itself. Education, which has in it the ingredients that will cause the person to be able to "think," vote and work for the common good is cut severely. This takes a caring person who has deep spiritual values that causes him/her to strive to understand both the greatest assets and the deficiencies in a society.

In such things as having good things for ourselves, we must see the nation's poverty, homelessness, hunger or the lack of the ordinary things which redound to the good and the upliftment of others. These are the sort of people who bring about the kind of thinking and action that says "ours" over "mine." Therefore, they have both sympathy and empathy for those who are "down and out." The sign of greatest good in these persons is seen in that they are there for both those who are in trouble or living a troubled life through no fault of their own but they also reach out to the errant ones who cause their own downfall. The Church must always keep this before the public, both private and public sectors.

The errant ones who Jesus had in mind when he said, "You have heard that it was said, you shall love your neighbor and hate your enemy. But I say to you love your enemy and pray for those who persecute you so that you may be like your Father who is in Heaven (a perfect society) for he makes his sun to rise on the <u>evil</u> and the <u>good</u> and sends his rain on the just and the unjust alike" (Matthew 5:43-45). This is not a saying that tells persons how to be "lawful" but a saying that is to let us all know who the great people are around us and imitate them— those who have conviction not from their own achievement but from their love toward other human beings. This gives all a chance--those who wrote the "Contract with America" and those who are the victims of it and may suffer from it.

When the "Religious Right" through their private press and the general communication media to which they have access quote the Scripture to get over their point of view, they are careful to see that the teaching of Jesus and some of the main Prophets are left out of their downgrading of the poor. They have such voices as Pat Robertson, James Buchanan to join with William Bennett, the former Secretary of Education, to downgrade what they call the "Liberals" to say the society has been misguided in helping the poor through the national aid. They contend that the poor should help themselves, an argument that none can gainsay. It is very popular to say that people should have a job and work for a living. But it is unpopular to say that we must have safety nets to see that the persons that "cannot" get jobs and who are not able to work, plus families with children who cannot get the kind of jobs that will bring them above the poverty line, should have a safety net. These never quote the Social Prophets such as Amos, Micah, Isaiah and, yes, Jesus. These persons' words do not break through to the public media. They stand and blame others when we all are the <u>others</u> who are to help lift the poor out of their poverty.

The shock of poverty will come into the thinking of caring people of the United States and the other Americas and they will not stand by an let people suffer in abject poverty because some politicians in Washington use the poverty stricken to make political gain for themselves by attacking the previous administrations which made valiant efforts to aid the poor and paved the way for millions to be lifted from poverty through education and other special aids. It has been our Federal System, our One Nation Under God, which has collectively worked for our freedoms, of which one was the "freedom from want." We need to refine and update our social system to help and satisfy our needs as a whole. But we take a backward step in our help when we are going back to "<u>Block Grants</u>," which is the "<u>States Rights</u>" method of distribution. The poorer States and the Provential Prejudices will be seen to rise again.

The Contract with America, as it speaks to the poor, is subtly but surely saying that the United States government should forsake the poor and the ones who "commit crimes" and the ones who have children out of wedlock. This subtle devastation of the poor is shown most pointedly in the cases in the Contract. Let us start with <u>Welfare</u>.

Under "Welfare Reform" the Contract starts out with the sentence, "Isn't it time for the government to encourage work rather than rewarding dependency? ...our Contract with America will achieve what some thirty years of massive welfare spending has not been able to accomplish: reduce illegitimacy, <u>require work</u>, and save tax payers' money."[3] This starts out with the proposition that people have not been encouraged to work before. This just is not true.

There are several defects in this section that spells out the heart of the mischief and the fallacies of the basic premise of the "Contract with America." First, the great fallacy that the States will do a better job in just receiving the "Block Grants" and telling them to determine the eligibility of the person who receives welfare. I would remind the persons who are the projectors of the Contract that this is the old bugaboo, "States Rights." That is, that the States can do everything better "far off" from the bureaucratic Central Government at Washington. This is both naïve and arrogant, if believed. If this form of naivete is coming from the chief law makers of our country, we are in deep trouble. They are dealing with age-old subjects which have come to us from the beginning of time but have been accentuated in our modern society by many social factors. Let us take the word "illegitimacy" and let us put beside it children that were born into a monogamous family which has the mother and father there to teach the culture— both values and activities— "til death do us part." This is an ideal situation depicting a world that never was. In the ancient days there was polygamy, where many women were cohabiting with one man. The children sometimes shared a system of tribal or group living. Then in the emigration to the Western world there was a predominance of males who mixed with the natives. This has happened with the male of the human species wherever they went. Then in American slavery, there was a tripod mixture. The tribal life was broken up and what we called the "Christian

---

[3] "Contract with America" pp. 65-77.

11

marriage" of monogamy was rare indeed. Families were sold, father from children and mothers, and sometimes even mothers from their children, and children from their mothers. Then there was the "White male" who fathered children by Black women; this was prevalent then. There was also the occasion when White women bore the children of Black men. Would we call all of these offspring illegitimate? <u>All</u> <u>children</u> <u>who</u> <u>come</u> <u>into</u> <u>the</u> <u>world</u> by whomever they are begotten are legitimate as they came through the God-given natural process. I am sure if the people who so glibly talk about illegitimacy (or as the former society used to say, <u>bastards</u>), if they would trace their family tree, would find that their genes and their very route of coming here had passed down the same road.

We are all here in this world, we are all persons of infinite worth, not made by birth or society. But as was spoken long ago and must be spoken now, "That which God has cleansed you must not call common or unclean" (Acts 10:14). This was a lesson that God had to teach Simon Peter, being a Jew, before he sent him to the Gentile Cornelius.

If we watch television, if we go to the movies, if we read newspapers or if we look around us, we will see, if we look in Washington, the House of Representatives or the Senate, we will not find "sexual purity." Or if we could learn to be truthful and fair with our children, they would live better lives sexually and otherwise.

There was a time when it was scandalous for a girl to have a child out of wedlock. There was also a time when it was scandalous for a man and wife to get a divorce. Those days are gone. Then, we ought to help our young people and not crush them for what we have taught them and for practicing the practices of the society in which they live.

Teenagers Do Not Get Babies In Order To Get Welfare Checks! They get babies due to a natural God-given appetite. We should teach them by word and example how to lead a sex life that will produce spiritual fulfilment which goes beyond physical pleasure. We should start marrying <u>one</u> <u>spouse</u> <u>for</u> <u>life</u> if we believe in this way of life.

What can the State do about illegitimacy? This is something that has been in all societies throughout the ages. But is the cure to take the children from the parents and put them in public custody and bring back the "Oliver Twist" kind of treatment? Is keeping the mother in school and also teaching young women how to raise children a much better solution? What about fathers? What is the way to teach the fathers a lesson? Is it better to put them in prison for punishment for non-child support or is it better to have them learning how to make good in a high technical society? What is the Church's, religious and civil institutions' role in this?

Jesus had some specific things to say to us about children. To take a child from his/her mother because she is a teenager or to let her/him and the child go hungry because of the way the child got into the world is not a "Contract with America" but a contract with the evil forces of the world. God still speaks to us about children. As Jesus says, "Truly, I say to you, unless you turn (from your ways) and become like children, you will never enter the Kingdom of Heaven. (You will not know how wonderful earth is.) Whoever humbles himself like this child, (he/she) is the greatest in the Kingdom. Whoever receives one such child in my name receives me; but whoever causes one of these little ones to sin, it would be better for him/her to have a millstone tied around his/her neck and drowned in the depth of the sea" (Matthew 18:3-5). All of this is said without asking who were the fathers or mothers.

No, Mr. and Mrs. "Contractors with America"—this time meaning the Americas, including the U.S.A.—the people of our enlightened age will not let you cripple or enslave our children to the past actions of the unenlightened even with your "block grants" to the States. Some of our States and their leaders have not gotten over the "Slaveocracy mind" of the past. They still try to block "voting rights," have a "fast justice system" in our courts against young men of color and in many other ways keep them from achieving. It was the States which had this nation to bleed and many to die by the thousands to hold on the idea that it was "the right" of each "State" in the Union to take all rights from Blacks, or Negroes, then later African Americans. It was the States that had the right to keep Blacks and women from democratic participation in their own destiny by denying them the right to vote. This vote is fundamental in self-determination in a representative democratic society in which the "Contract" says it believes.

We will see now that after the Congress has passed the welfare bill which grants the money to the States for welfare, the States will not be able to have "work fare" and other measure to dent the poverty among us. This is because the States will not be able to some unwilling to set up educational programs and placement programs to give the poor work at a living wage or help the children in this system.

When the Civil War was over there came about a coalition of Blacks and Whites (made up mostly of poor non-gentry) who made Reconstruction a feasible, workable process for freedom for all. Out of this came a new order

14

of things, expressed in the 13th, 14th and 15th Amendments to the Constitution, which when added to the Bill of Rights found a new status for all (with the exception of women until the 19th Amendment as late as 1920).

William M. James

The 13th Amendment (1865)

Neither Slavery nor involuntary servitude, except for punishment for crime, whereof the Party has been duly convicted, shall exist within the United States, or any place subject to their jurisdiction.

Section 2 – Congress shall have power to enforce this article by appropriate legislation.

The 14th Amendment 1868)

Section 1 – All parties born or naturalized in the United States and subject to its jurisdiction thereof, are citizens of the United States and of the State wherein they reside. No State shall make or enforce any law which shall abridge the privileges or immunities of Citizens of the United States nor shall any State deprive any person of life, liberty or property, without due process of law, nor deny to any person within its jurisdiction the equal protection of the laws.

Section 3 – The validity of public debt of the United States, authorized by law, including debts incurred for payment of pensions and bounties for services in suppression, insurrection or rebellion shall not be questioned. But neither the United States nor any State shall assume or pay any elect or obligation incurred in aid of insurrection or rebellion against the United States, or claim for loss or the emancipation of any slave, but all such debts, obligations and claims shall be illegal and void.

17

The 15th Amendment (1870)

The right of Citizens of the United States to vote shall not be denied or abridged by the United States or by any State on account of race, color or previous condition of servitude.

Section 2 – Congress shall have power to enforce this article with appropriate legislation.

The 19th Amendment (1920)

The right of citizens of the United States to vote shall not be abridged by the United States or by any State on account of sex. Congress shall have power to enforce this article by appropriate legislation.

The reason for writing out these Amendments in depth is because I read that in the 1994 Congress (Contract with America), an amendment to the Crime Bill was made by a Congressman (I think testing for the ridicule). This addition to the bill placed an Amendment from the Bill of Rights. The 4th Amendment was presented verbatim and was voted down 200 plus to 100 plus. Therefore, the Congress and the people should read the Constitution more often and closely. One can see that these Amendments were to protect the individual against the State, or whatever tier of government. If we look at history, it was the States that have been more likely to chip away freedoms of the individual, on the account of the closeness to the basic prejudices found in "so called" race, class, sexual orientation and sexuality of their being.

When we look at Reconstruction and the real progress being made back from the 1860's to the 1990's, then we see the rise of the "White male" power among the so-called gentry through the "Ku Klux Klan," the "White Caps," "Bull Dozers" and other oppressive groups. We see them take back the power and give it to the "States Rights" element; through lynching and slaughter and by taking the courts and all government agencies. They also nullified the 13th, 14th and 15th Amendments. The 13th by peonage, the 14th by taking over the courts, and the 15th by passing laws to nullify, and by the power of the shotgun and hanging rope.

William M. James

<u>The Ever-Present Danger</u>

The Declaration of Independence and the Constitution as amended have laid down for us a broad and solid foundation for individual liberty. We had better connect these with our heritage of the Judeo-Christian concepts of the worth of the human individual. These documents and doctrines have brought us to appreciate the gifts of God through the struggles of history for these fathomless gifts, part of which we now enjoy. This has been a progressive track as humankind has climbed upward. But now we should set our heads, hearts and faces toward the completion and fulfillment of all that was intended and pointed to by those who laid the foundation and pointed the way that coming generations should be headed. Our unending song should be, "No turning back, No turning back."

One of the dangers of the moderns is the gullibility of those great numbers who believe the propaganda of the instruments of modern media (can attract). That is, how easy it is for radio, records, television and now the "computer-managed information highway!" Can sway us. We and our whole nation can become victims of our material gadgets. Instead of our controlling them, they may control us. They will rob us of our freedom in the name of helping us to control our own destiny if we do not know something of the foundation of our nation and the blood, the toil and even the martyrs who gave of themselves to bring us this far on our way. Slick sayings such as the "Contract with America" can become a gimmick to rob us of the "freedom and justice for all" and give the power to "turn back the clock" and place our destiny in the hands of

21

a few. The unexplained cliché can trip us up as we view our personal well-being over and against our broader social interest in the body politics, of all of our fellow humans. We hear such words and phrases as "liberal, "conservatives," "tax payers' money," "your best interest," "saving you money," "government waste," "big government," "welfare cheats," and many others. We can begin to believe that these are our friends and we must vote for them. This comes to be a trite reason for voting for one. It is said that some of the persons who are hired to put together "slick sayings" are really the Madison Avenue-type "hawkers."

Two of the dangerous cliches of the Contract with America and other non-progressive groups who use the word "conservative" to describe themselves are "Block Grants" and "Affirmative Action." They are for the first and against the second.

Block Grants. In all of the basic philosophies of the Contract, this is the most subtle and the most dangerous. It is subtle because its historical context may not be understood. It is dangerous because it takes us back to battles already fought and thought won. It goes to the heart of what we call "Constitutional Government" framed on the rights of the individual as framed in the Declaration of Independence. Some of the founding fathers had similar ideas concerning humanity and how this humanity of individual freedom through this Republic should come to bear on 'humankind." Jefferson, James Madison and John Marshall would become three of the "center stage" players in this drama of life. Jefferson had penned the Declaration of Independence which was one of the "milestone" documents of history. He was a naturalist-deist who saw creation and the power behind it to be the factors from which society must take its cues if that society or nation was to succeed. He wrote the basic draft of this document stating that the reasons for the independence of nations were in order that the independence of the individual may be secure, not by the whims of humankind or the rules of society but by the basics and fundamentals of the Creator who had made all persons equal. He, in a part of this declaration, scourged King George III of England for snatching the persons from Mother Africa to bring them into slavery in the colonies. When this draft was rejected by the delegates he did not go the mat for this section; not that he was for slavery but that he believed that the natural process of humankind made them "good" and that slavery would be overthrown. As he states later in his autobiography, he believed that the closer government got to the people, the people would be fair and adjudicate each other in humanistic affairs.

But there was a special group of the Federalists that believed that the protection of the individual had to be by the powers of the Federal Constitution. Among these were John Marshall who became the Chief Justice of the Supreme Court and James Madison, among others. Marshall had a kind of distrust for the idea that the State and local governments would be better protectors of the individual rights than the Constitution as framed by the Congress as an impartial document. He saw this as the people's security. He, with Madison and other Federalists, believed that the strength of the national government was better for the individual than the provincialism which would be found in the State governments. Jefferson, Marshall and Madison were all for the "Rights" of "Man," or the individual, but had different ways of approaching it. During their lifetime and later, the issue of "States Rights" became acute because of the Southern States' support of slavery and the spreading of slavery in new States. There came the rise of John C. Calhoun of South Carolina, the pillow on "States Rights." On the Federalist side was Daniel Webster, with Henry Clay as mediator. The Compromise of 1820, the Missouri Compromise, and the Compromise of 1850 accentuated the battle between "States Rights" and the Federal system. But behind it all hung slavery like the sword of Damocles with "King Slavery's" throng being ever in danger of being toppled through the Federal process. This was true because the basic freedom set by universal standards of the Declaration of Independence could not be justified as long as slavery existed. The only argument left was to dehumanize the persons enslaved. This process of dehumanizing the Black people, the main tenets of slavery in the Western world, was projected as a solution. Therefore, a false anthropology was tried. This was hard to justify when a look at history was brought into the equation. The "Slaveocracy" ignored history and appealed to the base instinct of the unlearned, and out of this came the words "white supremacy," "the white man's burden," "leaders by the evolutionary process," "manifest destiny" and other phrases to justify this slavery which stood out against the Declaration of Independence. Then there came, through Calhoun and others, the phrase "States Rights." This was a clause in the 10th Amendment of the Constitution giving the smaller units of the government certain rights to protec themselves from the tyranny of the Federal government.

We must remember that the revolutionary war had been fought over the tyranny of the "Divine Rights of Kings." But this caution never meant that the "States" had the rights to become the despotic group or to become tyrannical over the individual. But this was what "States Rights" came to mean by the Calhouns and his ideological offspring. The State had rights to do with the individual as it made laws and rules to treat those within its territories. This clashed with the "Declaration of Independence" which said the basic rights of the individual was a <u>universal right</u> written at the very heart of creation, or the universe, and by the Creator and not through the documents of a given government or society. Therefore, the Declaration of Independence was a document to bring about a society that would form its rules and laws to fit this fixed position, by the Creator of the universe, of the position the human individual should hold or have in that society; that the Creator had been even-handed in the creative process, making all persons equal.

As I have said, Jefferson and John Marshall believed that these rights should be secure. But they differed in the warp and means by which the society should carry them out. But on the other side was Calhoun, whose position denied the fundamentals of the Declaration in his "States Rights" argument, in that he gave the "States" the "rights" to fix the destination of the individual and to fix the definition of which the individual should be protected by the rule of law and which should not. This was an escape hatch for slave owners.

Throughout the history of this nation the believers in the Declaration of Independence have used it to project the basic freedoms of the individual in laws and rules projected in human rights. While on the other hand, the "States Rights" believers have used "States Rights" too many times to "take away" or to fail in yielding to the universal principles of "Human Rights."

This dichotomy of positions has been the dividing point of this nation from the beginning. It has been the dividing point in the justice system, the economic system, the education system, commercial system and others. The Supreme Court from John Marshall to Thurgood Marshall; and from Roger Taney to Clarence Thomas and Antonin Scalia has taken two sides of this argument. The 1896 Court's "separate but equal" and the 1954 Earl Warren Court's "separate is inherently unequal" has wrestled between finding law and freedom under the Declaration of Independence as included in the Constitution. The close connection between law of human society and "strict construction" of the Constitution and the wider meaning of "natural rights" of humanity of the Declaration of Independence have clashed throughout the history of this nation. But thanks be to God that the natural or the "God given" rights of the individual seems to be winning whenever the society is most democratic and the societal or "contracted" rights win when the society is most tyrannical or autocratic.

This matter was the prime cause of the Civil War. The "War Between the States" as the Calhoun followers would call it in defense of "States Rights." The "War of Rebellion" as Abraham Lincoln called it in defense of "one nation under God, with liberty and justice for all." He always quoted the Declaration of Independence and scripture in his arguments.

As I have said, from 1896 "Separate but Equal" to "Affirmative Action" under Lyndon Johnson and California's Proposition 902 of 1996, the battle still rages on and on. From the Roosevelt administration through the Carter administration, "individual rights" seemed be winning. But when the Nixon administration was able to win the "Southern Democratic" or "Dixiecrats" over to the Republican party, the rights of the individual seemed to be in the balance. The winning of President Clinton for a second term has a meaning for the nation, but the battle is to be joined in the twenty-first century.

The "universal rights" seems to be gaining ground but being attacked under the so-called "Christian Right" which would be better named the "Religious Right," not after the name of Christ who was <u>the</u> leader in individual freedom and universal endowment by God as the Father of all who gives these rights. The "Religious Right would fit more into the "States Rights" that fits into the powers of the few.

We say that labels will not give us a true picture of persons who fight for the "higher roads" of our society. But their action or performance will show them as they are: "You will know Christians by their love" and this is shown in action.

What we must not do is to let the framers of the Contract with America back us into a past which the progress and the forward-looking people have not witnessed or researched. If we do we will find ourselves in an eighteenth and nineteenth century mold which will prevent this nation from the rightful place as a leader for the twenty-first century. We must not hail the Contract's concepts as dead. It is only in its cocoon stage, going through the winter of the Clinton landslide, waiting to break forth to bring the terror of the past to individual freedom.

During the Roosevelt administration the ethnic groups and the so-called "racial groups"--especially the Blacks and the rising Hispanic population—began to regain some of these rights. We then had the Vincent and the Warren Supreme Courts and Justices like Judge "Whitest Wearing"

27

of South Carolina (who gave the decision that the Democratic primary must be open to Blacks because it was a part of the election process). Then came the pressure of the Civil Rights Movement, carried on by a coalition of groups: the N.A.A.C.P. (National Association for the Advancement of Colored People, the mother/father of the advocate organization for Blacks, made up of Whites and Blacks), the Urban League (which did much more for the migrant population of Blacks moving into the urban centers), C.O.R.E. (Congress on Racial Equality, led by James Farmer as a protest organization), and SNCC (Students Non-violent Coordinating Committee), one of the greatest student organizations which this nation has seen (made up of Blacks and Whites until the Black Nationalists took it over and killed it). Then there were the churches which had always been in the forefront in leading movements of upliftment. Out of the churches came the SCLC (Southern Christian Leadership Conference) led by the great prophet and sage Martin Luther King Jr. In the 'Contract" the name of President Lyndon B. Johnson is mentioned. But what it did not say about Lyndon Johnson, Southerner and Texan, was that he <u>broke</u> <u>the</u> <u>power</u> of the filibuster. He linked up with Everett McKinley Dirkson (Republican from Illinois) and Hubert Horatio Humphrey and they were able to lift the Constitution back on track from its ditching in 1896 by the Supreme Court's "separate but equal" ruling. He was able to say, "We shall overcome" and to also say that "If you give the Blacks the vote then they will take care of the rest."

President Johnson saw that the lack of economic opportunity through the robbery of the Blacks from starting the race of life from a fair point was a tremendous handicap. The economic "make ups" would depend on the society's help. Out of this came the idea of the "Great Society" and the "War Against Poverty." The people of the"Contract" cannot see how much has been gained from these days of struggle. These named people are heroes in the struggle in this nation for a democratic society. We could say that Lyndon B. Johnson fought for a great society. Out of this came "Affirmative Action."

I would like to point out to the people in the Contract that these are recent happenings, the right to vote, affirmative action for education and for jobs, the right to live in housing in one's choosing and the ability to pay for it, the right to go to many schools and universities paid for by taxpayers' money. I am at the age that I have seen all the oppression and the achievements in spite of it. Some of us know when the State built fine high schools for Whites and many communities had "no" high schools for Blacks and we were expected to rise by our "boot straps" when we did not have the boots or the straps.

Many of the signatures of the Contract were here and alive when much of the disparities were in place; much worse, when the State had taken the right to vote and had enforced laws of "separate but equal," where the separate was enforced but the equal was forgotten and only thirty years ago was restored.

The United States that I know and in which I have grown up and worked is not a mean-spirited country but the people are generous and willing to give of themselves if given a chance. Many immigrants and migrants have not forgotten the struggle of the aliens. They remember the stories handed down to them and that they were called "wops," "dagoes," "greasers," "red necks," "poor white trash," "niggers," "nigger lovers," and we could go on and on. This is not America or the United States at its best.

The shining hours of the United States have been displayed by its saints and martyrs and heroes such as William Lloyd Garrison; Wendell Philips; John Brown before being hanged at Harpers Ferry; Julia Ward Howe in the "Battle Hymn of the Republic; Lincoln, over the noble dead at Gettysburg, Pennsylvania and in his second inaugural address; James Weldon Johnson in his poem "Lift Every Voice and Sing"; Franklin Delano Roosevelt in his "We have nothing to fear but fear itself" from which we still hear the echoes; Martin Luther King Jr. and his "I have a Dream" Speech and its climatic "I have been to the mountain top"; and thousands who have bled and died for the freedom and liberty we hold so dear.

So we shall not be turned from a caring nation – caring about all of God's world. I would rather hear Emma Lazarus, the great Jewish philanthropist, female poet who set a higher and nobler tone for the United States of America than any political 'Contract" can ever blot out when she wrote the heart of the reality of our creed under God, by saying:

> Not like the brazen giant of Greek fame,
> With conquering limbs astride from land to land;
> Here at our sea-washed sunset gates shall stand
> A mighty woman with torch, whose flame
> Is the imprisoned lightning, and her name,
> Mother of Exiles, From her beaconed-hand
> Flows worldwide welcome; her mild eyed command
> The air bridged harbor that twin cities frame.
>
> Keep ancient lands, your storied pomp she cries
> With silent lips, 'Give me your tired, your poor,

Your huddled masses yearning to be free,
The wretched refuse of your teaming shore,
Sent these, the homeless, tempest-tossed to me,
I lift my lamp beside the golden door.'

Emma Lazarus (1848-1887)

This was inscribed at the base of the Statue of Liberty. This sentiment was the foundation of those born by toil, tears and joys of this country. So they come from Africa, Asia, Europe, and the isles beyond the sea. This is the United States of America, this is the America which no written document shall be able to blot it out from germination which came from the hand of God, the flame or the torch of liberty has come through wars, floods and flame and will remain our heritage under God. The poor will always be of interest to us. We say as Lincoln said, "God must love the poor for he made so many of them." Watch my word, the poor will learn to vote!

William M. James

The next item of the Contract is that 'it will require work.'

There is no lack of the desire to work in our society. There are and have been some lazy people in every society but this is not the real problem of our unemployed and underemployed. There is and there will be under our present system a shortage of jobs and a lack of education and skilled training for many of the jobs which exist. T. S. Eliot in his drama-poem "Choruses from the Rock" says, "The lot of man is ceaseless labor, or ceaseless idleness, which is harder or irregular labor, which is not pleasant." Then he has the voices of the unemployed answer in the chorus, "No man has hired us, with pocketed hands and lowered faces, we stand about in open places, shiver in unlit rooms, where only the wind moves. Our empty fields, untilled, where the plow rests at an angle to the furrow. In this land, there shall be one cigarette to two men, to two women one half pint of bitter ale. In this land no man has hired us. Our life is unwelcome, our death unmentioned in 'The Times.'"[4] Eliot's idea here comes from the parable of Jesus. Jesus tells a story of householder who went out to hire persons in the early morning and he hired what he needed. He went back later and he hired another crew, and still later he went by and saw a group standing idle and he asked, "Why do you stand here idle all day?" They said to him, "Because no one has hired us." He took them and gave them work. When the time came for pay he rewarded

---

[4] T.S. Eliot's Complete Works – Choruses from the Rock, pp. 97, 99.

them all the same. Jesus was saying, the need of people is the way it is done in the Kingdom of God.

We need to have some "kingdom" economics in our land. The highest value in "The Contract with America" has been placed on money. We have made money have intrinsic worth. We blasted Russia for its materialistic society, while putting money above all other values in our society. We have placed money above our children, our education system, above our elderly, above our arts and culture, and above the very value systems of life in which we glibly say we believe. In the parable of the kingdom, Jesus makes the value or the need of the worker higher than the money given to each.

I hear our governor, our mayor, and many elected officials saying, "What we need is to put people to work. Work is what people need, so let's create jobs." Good, I say, but is this realistic or political propaganda? Do we really believe that if every able-bodied person were trained and ready for work that society as now organized would have jobs for all? If we believe, this we have not assessed the technology and the coming technology of the twenty first century. Which is upon us now.

The ploy of the States under the new welfare "Block Grants System" seems to be aimed at getting the people off welfare to work at public works and private "hire outs" at about the same amount of money or less than they were getting on welfare. This would leave them still in poverty where they were locked in low-paying jobs which would not provide the incentives to work in order that they would advance economically to break their bonds of poverty.

The above could bring about two negative results. One, persons could supplement their low pay by getting illegitimate income through drug-selling, prostitution, gambling and other negatives. This would lead their status to be some degrees below what it is at the present time and accentuate the crime springing from these activities. Second, this could cause them to remain in their impoverished position with children growing up in a continuing poverty cycle which would lead them to be anti-social when they understand their helpless state.

The welfare bill is a tremendous gamble for this nation. Contrary to the political propaganda after the War on Poverty which began in 1965 under the Johnson administration, the poverty of children below eighteen years of age fell some 33-1/2 percent. In 1965 the census showed the number to be 14.7 million children under the poverty line. This had dropped to 9.8 million in the next ten years. When there were built-in educational benefits and other training programs for people eighteen to thirty years old, there was a drop in the whole social plight. Both the inflation rate and the interest rate on the national debt, which jumped sharply in the last twelve years, have effected our economy. The politics by propaganda would place the rise on the welfare and the entitlement programs for the poor. This does not fit the reality of the neutral economist's figures. The cut in taxes while carrying almost a century of war-time debts plus the heavier spending on future war weapons which were beyond our needs, this plus the transition from an industrial age to the age of automation, has had and is having great effects on our work force, especially entry level and manual labor jobs which we had in the Industrial Revolution. It would have been much better if we would acknowledge this fact and set up a commission of industrial and economic planners to look at our work for the future days and the fact that we will have more idle time. How shall we divide our time in order that

<u>everyone will have a living wage and know how to use</u> <u>leisure time. This is the kind of world we are heading</u> <u>toward.</u>

The fact is there has always been through the tiers of government structure some checks on welfare cheats. What is needed is to keep these checks and to build more opportunity through public jobs (real jobs), extensive demanded training for jobs in the public and private sectors, and job placement centers for processing and placement plus more child care centers for working parents.

We live in a society where certain magazines, such as Forbes, come out each year showing how many billionaires and the number of multi-millionaires the nation has. Then that large population who live under the poverty line sees this and looks at television and sees the material riches of the nation both in the potential and actual wealth piled up. Then one wonders about the "haves." How can so few have so much and so many have so little? These "have nots" are not going into a philosophical analysis as to why this is. They are just going to say that there is "something wrong." This becomes sort of the "not caring" about the social whole. This is the basis of much of the unrest and fear in our society. We have lost our sense of caring and planning.

Our work attitudes and our scale of pay for work have a great deal to do with our crime rate. The pointed dagger beams or shines on the "Black Males" in our country. They are no more addicted to crime than any other segment in our society but they have less opportunities for jobs which elevate them to higher places in society. There are certain other deficiencies in our society that have mediated to the downfall of many of our young Black and Hispanic males.

Some time ago I was invited to attend the Alex Haley farm in Tennessee. The Children's Defense Fund asked me to give a paper on "The Church and the Black Male." Following are excerpts from the paper presented,

William M. James

The Revitalization of the Black Male Through the Christian Church[5]

"I start out on this positive note and write that something can happen and should happen to undergird Black males to achieve their best. They have the potential and latent power to make the nation and the world a better place and find fulfillment in doing so.

First, we would like to ask ourselves questions about Black young men from the deep-seated negatives of our society. The question is generally, 'What's wrong with Black young men today?" This question is often wrongly put in our time. The question should be, 'What is wrong with our society today that is producing so much chaos among our Black young people?' (I could just say "young people," for millions of all kinds find themselves lost in our time.)

We deal with statistical data and by samples, and sadly shake our heads at what the statistical facts tell us. That is, that one-fourth of all of our Black males are incarcerated or on probation or parole, but all of these have been before the courts for some misdeed which they have committed or may have committed. We bring out other statistics to bear on our plight – one, that most of the crimes by these young people are drug related.

---

[5] William James, Presentation to the Conference on Fostering Wholesome Development and Rehabilitation of African American Males.

We also show that the preponderance of violence perpetrated by Black young men is on Blacks. Then the statistician begins to take over our thought and reasoning powers. Then we trot out some of the most devastating statistics, that forty percent plus of Black males drop out of school between the ninth and tenth grades; read on the fourth and fifth grade levels; from twenty to twenty-five percent of our young Black males are unemployed and another fifteen to twenty percent are underemployed (not making enough money to keep their families above the poverty line). We continue that some forty percent of teen-aged girls have babies out of wedlock. This is from unions with the same young men who we have discussed in the various conditions.

Therefore, we let the statisticians control our attitudes and behavior among and toward our young men. We do not go back to the causes or reasons that these happenings are going on among us. We take the statistical facts as the true conditions of our young people. We have something which "goes off" or explodes down deep that says these young people ought to do better than this. We say this without asking why or how. Or better, What! We do not ask ourselves what our role is in all of this. We stand clear of both blame and salvation and say someone else should correct this. We act as if we believe that our young people should come up 'smelling like roses'."

The Great Migration

"The people of the migration that took place during and after the First and Second World Wars were Blacks from the south. They went to the midwest and the eastern seaboard. They brought with them the ideas of industry, education for their young people and religion. The central hope in all of this movement was the Black Church. The Church had specialized in building private schools for learning, both secondary and higher educational institutions. They saw these as the badge of hope and evidence of success for Black people. The churches of various denominations followed the people, or were in some way already established in these cities. Mainly the churches were Baptist, Methodist of various kinds, a limited number of Presbyterians and Congregationalists. The Holiness and Pentecostal Churches were just beginning to take hold in significant numbers among Black people.

The migrants went to the churches of their choice. The main civic organizing was conducted by the NAACP and the Urban League. Both got most of their members from the church. To belong to them was a badge of insurance for basic social living, education and moral stability. These people had come out of a tradition of an organized society in the midst of a larger sometimes hostile society. They organized their own organizations such as burial societies, the church clubs of various types and other organizations from the patterns gleaned from their former homes. The Christian Church was their stabilizing influence.

The first and second generations followed the leads of the church. Great pastors, as shepherds of their flocks, rose up to become moral and civic leaders that affected the whole of city life. The Sunday Schools of the churches were the bastions of moral and ethical teachings. It was almost a scandal for a child to stay out of Sunday School.

Most of the time, the class and economic differences broke down at the church doors and a leveling took place. Doctor so-and-so became Brother so-and-so. They had come out of a tradition of helping one another, especially helping the young people to go to colleges and other types of schools. The Church had a fellowship that was found nowhere else in the society. This was a place of social gatherings where many of the civic and community plans were made, where courtships were formed, out of which grew marriage and families. It was here that political plans were made and the intergroup coordination was set up to elect persons of color to offices in order to gain in the Black community.

Then there began to be an elitist group who began to think that the Church was not sophisticated enough for its general ideas to save the society. These began to think that the Church was for those who sang and prayed but the action was always outside. Where in the past the Church had been the very factor that built the colleges, set the conditions for the privileged operation, now the Church began to be for "certain types" of persons. Therefore, within the Church the more sophisticated began to act like those outside of the Church. The moral codes and teachings of the Church began to break down to imitate the society in general.

This change was taking place at a rapid pace in the Thirties and Forties. In the past the mainstream of Protestants, Baptists and Methodists especially taught against church members drinking alcoholic liquors, smoking, swearing and using profanity. The new breed of Christian began to ignore those. The newest denominations among us, the Pentecostal and Holiness types began to imitate the Roman and the fundamentalist theology – that was to "put fear in the hearts" of people. God became one to fear and escape from His wrath. This changed the whole outlook from the "<u>Christ that set you free</u>" and the theology of our foreparents who had been steeped in the idea that it was God through Christ who was the 'father' figure. <u>It was He who had power to overcome the oppressor</u>. The "fear factor" did not stand up under the scrutiny of the new look at freedom and higher education. Therefore, this kind of God was becoming irrelevant to so many of our young educated. Even those who belonged to the Church took it as a "Sunday thing" and not relevant to the realities to the economic "work-a-day" world.

In the late Thirties and Forties, there was a movement that seemed to promote "cultic" churches. (Some were called "Christians" and other had other names.) They were generally built around "cultic" leaders. Some names are very familiar, such as Father Divine who had his Heavens, Prophet Jones, Daddy Grace, Rev. Becton, Elder Michaux and others. (These persons seemed to fare well economically.) Then there came a shift since the use of the name "Church" and "Christian" had been well over-exploited. Then there came the name of Mohammed (and Islam). This was a counter action to the exploitation of the name "Jesus." There also was the more secular Black Nationalist Movement. The concept was based on so-called "Race" and emphasized "Blackness," and had both charm and power. Black became "beautiful" in itself and the clenched raised fist became the symbol of "Black Power."

Some of these movements were for exploitation and "far out" in their applications. Others were honestly conceived but to the counteraction of the truth of the precondition of the White majority. But all left a confused condition in which our young men were to grow up. They were in a maze. As these movements grew, the "Afro-centric" movement became confused. In going back to the roots of Black people in Africa in the sixteenth and seventeenth centuries, we neglected five hundred years of significant history of the African descendants and the contributions they had made in the Western world. One of these contributions had been the effects that the African people had on the Christian Church during and after slavery. They had also sent the theologians back to the First Century Church to look at patterns of a democracy in the Western world. The Church had set a pattern in the early centuries that was to result in eliminating slavery throughout the world whether in the form of indentured servitude or chattel slavery. This was put in the Declaration of Independence by Jefferson when he said, "We hold these truths to be self evident that all men (generic) are created equal and endowed by their Creator with certain inalienable rights. Among these are life, liberty and the pursuit of happiness." This has been the taking-off point for all of those who would defend the rights of the individual. This brought about a new struggle for freedom everywhere. But it stemmed from St. Paul's interpretation of the "Jesus way" of life, who said, "There are neither Jew nor Greek, there is neither slave nor freeman, neither male or female, for you are all one in Jesus Christ and if you are Christ's then you are Abraham's offspring, heirs according to the promise" (Galatians 3:38-29). This stems from the teaching of Christ in the Books of

Matthew and Luke. But its origin is from the promise or the covenant with Abraham in the Book of Genesis. In Genesis, 12th Chapter, first to third verses, it says, "Now the Lord said to Abraham, 'Go from your country and from your <u>kindred</u> (meaning blood kindred) and from your <u>father's</u> house (family) to the land that I will show you. And I will make you a great nation, and I will bless you and make your name great that you will be a blessing. <u>I will bless them who bless you</u> (who take your pattern of life), <u>I will curse them who curse you</u> and <u>by you all the families of the earth shall bless themselves</u>." This is what is called the <u>Old Covenant</u> or the Old Testament. Christ becomes the <u>New Testament</u> or Covenant. The reason that the Church has left these covenants is they wish to choose a way that will help themselves and not one which will bless the families of the earth.

It was the prophets of Israel who tried to call Israel back to the covenant or their reason for being and it was the Black Church and the Black people in the Western world whose reason for being was to bring us back to these fundamental truths of life; that is, that there are different cultures (how people grew up and what they take on from the society in which they grow). But there is only one humanity that shares the fundamental traits of humanity under one common creation. Without this fundamental concept of the infinite and endowed right of the human being, the human race is in serious trouble.

We now see this from the narrow point of view of the possibility of the extinction of the Black male but this possibility lingers over us all in a world where natural scientific inventions of destruction have outstripped the

45

humanities or the behavioral sciences of human aspiration and needs.

Some see the Christian Church as a solution and the failure of the Church as the cause. Some time ago we were in a meeting on youth services at what was then the Harlem YWCA. I made a statement on the floor. I said to the group that the only thing that will save Black youth was the Church. A man named Charles Kenyatta who had been one of Malcolm X's bodyguards got the floor. I wondered what he was going to say. He had been a leader of the Mau Maus. I and many others were wide-eyed with surprise when he said, "Reverent James is right. The only hope the Black young people have is the Church. If we let them miss that, all of us have missed the boat." This was at the height of the Black Nationalist ascendancy. Mr. Charles Kenyatta was soon to become the Reverend Charles Kenyatta.

Churches, so-named, might be "racist." But the Church of Christ is not racist wherever it is found. We make a great mistake when we play racism on a group or individual and perpetuate on a person or group because of their ethnic background. We might ask ourselves what causes racism? Well, it is something far deeper than just pointing out one group over another. There is something deeper than the surfaces of persons or systems "putting down" or persecuting people because of color or ethnic background. This is bad but it is not the prime cause of this. This is bad but there is something there in humanity that causes them to destroy their fellow human beings. This can be in the same ethnic group, the same family group, the same national group. People have always found a way to destroy one another with or without cause. We have taken out of our vocabulary the word "sin," or, that inner development of that selfishness that causes them to not really have love or empathy. The Church is neglecting the universal covenant of blessing the whole world. This is true whether the old or new covenant rises above ethnic or racial groups and moves toward humankind.

The loss of this basic thing in the Church is causing us to lose the young of the Church and send them out to a secular world because we in the Church have taken on a secular philosophy or theology."

The Contract and the Criminal Justice System

The "Contract" seems to see punishment as the main corrective of antisocial behavior. This is a fallacy that has been with us from the beginning of time; a method that has not worked but we keep on plugging away as if this is a cure-all for antisocial behavior. This filters down to persons and actually conditions their behavior and causes them to rebel against society at a greater pace. Some have tried the Christian way of rehabilitation; that is, to let the perpetrator know the real damage to others caused and to give him/her a way out of this kind of behavior. This can be done with stern action but without vindictiveness or hate of the person. One will have to understand that the person is still part of the human family, even if a bad one. One must also see that the person is redeemable. This is seen in our society only for the white collar criminals and sometimes even they are victims of the punishment process.

When the society falls into the "punishment-for-vindictiveness" or "making-an-example" method, everyone is in danger, even the very rich. Two examples of this are in the cases of Patty Hearst and Leona Helmsley. Both women are very rich but both fell into the "make-the-an-example" process. Each in the ordinary process would have brought a look at justice what would have been sympathetic—in the case of Ms. Hearst, reaching out to her for what she had gone through; in the case of Mrs. Helmsley, the probability of a "top" mistake with the admonition to "pay up" whatever penalties were imposed. But there had been so much publicity in both cases. Therefore, punishment became the "Justice Answer." Without the publicity, both women would have most likely received both sympathy and empathy from those around them, and gone free. Our justice system needs objective, even-handed justice for all.

As we have said, Black Hispanic and many young people are stigmatized as the "criminal type." This causes the police and many times the courts to have preconceived notions of the guilt of these young men before they ever come to trial. Therefore, the reverse of our legal system is applied. They are looked upon as guilty until they have proven themselves innocent instead of the standard of"justice for all," "innocent until proven guilty." If the signers of the Contract with America could follow the process of some of our State court systems from arrest to the "holding pens" (these are the places where persons are kept before their first hearing before the courts), they would be more sensitive to justice. When I was a pastor in New York City whenever one Black or Hispanic young man in our community was arrested, for any cause, I would rush to the police precinct or have someone else to go to let the police know that someone was following these youngsters to see that they were not brutalized. Many of the policemen or detectives were zealous in seeing that the young people were protected and their rights were upheld, but there were others, all too many, that would treat the youngsters with contempt and punish them with methods bordering on sadism. This is generally hidden from our public or our society. Therefore, it is the general belief that these young people "got what was coming" for they are "hoodlums" and the only way they learn is to "come down hard" on them. This method is counterproductive in every way. First, it causes many innocent young people to be unjustly punished and become the prime factors of the "revolving door" action of young people. The way to create patriotism in them is to promote a fair hearing starting with the police and the courts. We will see this will cause a response that will amaze us.

If we look at history we would find that some of the most brutal punishment came from Europe in the Middle Ages. The torture chambers did not stop crime but accentuated the hostility against those societies and even brought about physical rebellions and revolutions. There must be a faith in fairness in a society. When this is generally established we would see more loyalty is given to that society. Much of our crime springs from resentment of our society and hostility springs from the belief that it is unfair. If we would take statistics among the persons who went in prisons and never returned, a larger number would be from prisons where persons were treated humanely over and against those being brutalized as a part of the prison system.

In the "Contract," in addressing prevention measures, it again puts their applications of preventive programs in the hands of local officers. It says, "The proposed [meaning "our"] legislation will leave the discretion with local officers who are closest to the problem. Only they can determine their specific needs and solutions to address the crime in their communities. The proposed legislation asks only prevention programs involve law enforcement organizations and truly address the crime problems of that community. This is in clear contrast to the crime bill that contains billions of one-size-fits-all social welfare programs that have nothing to do with crime but are pork-barrel handouts to political cronies."[6] This would exclude prevention programs by other community organizations such as the Church and other social uplift organizations.

The people of the "Contract" seem to ignore history. This is an unthinkable thing to do. Do we ignore our background as a nation? This would be unthinkable since we are so young and recent in history. We have the test to achieve, we have a track record to make. Never in this history of civilization or the pre-history as we know it have we had such an array of ethnicity or mixed groups living together as a nation. Never has there been such a mixture of colors—as David Dinkins, the former mayor of New York City, calls it, the "great mosaic.". Never have so many cultures lived together in close proximity to one another. We are still being tested to see if "this nation or any nation can endure" with such a mixture. The racism which is ingrained in the United States of America's ethos affects the whole system. This part of our history we must seek to eliminate.

---

[6] Contract With America," p. 60.

The Contract With America versus The Covenant With God

If we would take a survey of all who signed the "Contract," each would declare that he/she is not a racist and far from it. If the same question was asked of most of the Ku Klux Klan members, the answer would be the same. If the same question was asked of any "Black Nationalist" or "new Israelite" who stand on street corners spewing racist venom at the "white man," the answer would be the same. All would state that they are coming from a position of truth or fact. Some would believe that they are right in their answer, some would not. But few would understand they are influenced by an ethos of racism in our nation.

In the last of the Thirties and in the early Forties, the late Newton D. Baker of the Carnegie Corporation set out to look at the whole racial structure in America. Andrew Carnegie had great interest in what was called the "Negro question." He had also given generously for "Negro education. He gave generously to Hampton Institute in Virginia and Tuskegee Institute in Alabama. Searching for a person to put the whole study together, they chose Dr. Gunnar Myrdal, a young scholar from Stockholm, Sweden. Dr. Myrdal had a reputation as a social economist and was an advisor to the Swedish government. He had also served in the Swedish senate. He put together one of the greatest teams to study racism that this or any other country had ever had. This study and contacts were made with the background of the rise of Hitler in Germany and in alarming effort of Nazism under Hitler to exterminate the Jews under the guise of keeping pure the "Master Race," or "Aryan Race."

In the "American Dilemma," Dr. Myrdal says,

> "The moralism and rationalism are for many of us—among them the author of this book—the glory

of the nation, its youthful strength, perhaps the salvation of mankind. The analysis of this 'American Creed' and its implication have an important place in our inquiry. While on the one hand, to such moralistic and rationalistic being as the ordinary American, the Negro problem and his own confused and contradictory attitudes toward it must be disturbing; on the other hand, the very mass of unsettled problems in his heterogeneous and changing culture and inherited liberalistic trust that things will ultimately take care of themselves and get settled one way or another, enabling the ordinary American to live on happily, with recognized contradictions around him and within him in a kind of bright fatalism, which is unmatched in the rest of the Western world. This fatalism also belongs to the National Ethos.
The American Negro's problem is a problem at the heart of the American. It is there that the interracial tension has its focus. It is there that the decisive struggle goes on. This is the central view point of this treatise. Though our study includes economic, social and political race relations, at the bottom our problem is a moral dilemma of the American—the conflict between the high moral valuation on various levels of consciousness and generosity."[7]

Then, we see that Dr. Myrdal sees our basic problem, as we are torn between our high moral ideals and our actual behavior toward one another where race is concerned, is the base of all other problems that spring from it in race

---

[7] Gunnar Myrdal, "American Dilemma," Introduction, p. xiiii

relations. He further implies that this dilemma effects every other section of our society.

The heart of the problem is a moral problem in which race plays an important part. The idea of equal acceptance on merit or grace is deeper than the political problem."" As Dr. Myrdal states, "The American Dilemma referred to in the title of this book is the ever-raging conflict between, on the one hand, the valuation preserved on the general plane which we shall call the "American Creed" where the American thinks, talks, and acts under the influence of high national and Christian concepts, and on the other hand, the valuation of specific planes of individual and group living where personal and local interest, economic, social and sexual jealousies, considerations of community prestige and conformity, group prejudice against particular persons or types of people, and all sorts of miscellaneous wants, impulses and habits dominate his outlook."

He further states that it was born out of the conflict between old harshly non-egalitarian institutions – which was not, or perhaps in a short time could not, be erased and a new shining faith in human liberty and democracy. Another accomplishment of early rationalistic enlightenment had laid the theoretical basis for the racial defense of slavery – until this philosophical basis was laid, racism was not an intellectual possibility.

What we have to consider is how does Congress or States or local communities begin to deal with the subtle prejudice which pervades our society as a whole and all of its parts. When we look at our media, it is there, our schools of learning, it is there; when we look at our supposedly purest institution, the Church, it is there. We find it among all who fail to <u>think</u> of persons to be of infinite worth. The leveling point is found in Christ's approach – as all coming from a common father – "Our father," "progenitor" or "Creator." This is very difficult to move from thinking "they" to "we." Some time ago we had a discussion with a young "African American," as we call him. He was very proud to say that human beings had their origin in Africa and had come from northeast Africa. He said it in a way that he thought should make "us" proud or even superior. Then I asked, who is this "us," since we all emerged from "one" common place. This seems to make us all "us." He said he had never looked at the problem this way. Many are ready to admit that it seems that we all have a common origin but it is hard for us to see that humanity is one and especially in our American background. We come from many cultures/the ethos in which we have developed over many thousands of years, offering our cultures into one common pool which we call civilization, our civilization being made up of all these cultures which makes us persons of an "eclectic" culture which has been brought to us by all groups.

In spite of all of this we find ourselves downgrading some of our groups, especially those easily identifiable, in order to make them lesser beings than ourselves.

<u>Our Congress and our Administration must rise above some of the "racial" and "ethnic" agenda to a higher look at all being from a common Creator.</u>

<u>"One nation under God."</u>

This is a quotation from Abraham Lincoln who grew to present this from his experience of this nation going through and down the path of fratricide and the elimination of itself. One may think that this battle was won once and for all. But no battle, to bring about unity among humanity, is won once and for all time during the "Civil War" or "rebellion." In a sense, each generation must fight this battle with different weapons but it must be fought.

There are those who would divide or Balkanize this nation into small units called States, with the powers or strength within each unit to stand as a unit within itself in everything except national defense. First, this is an impossibility and can be only mouthed by the politicians for their own personal benefit. Under our system we are citizens of one country, the "United States of America." This country guarantees each individual freedom and equality through the powers of a general Constitution which guarantees each citizen protection through this main Constitution in spite of any law or regulation to the contrary made by any State or smaller unit of government. There must be enough power behind this to see that this is enforced and enforced through interpretation by the Judiciary System, the highest being the Supreme Court, a part of the Federal System, and the Legislative System, the Congress, which has the duty to make laws and regulations within the bounds of the Constitution that will keep abreast with the times and adhere to the well-being of the citizens of the United States individually and collectively; and then the Executive System to see that all laws and regulations

William M. James

are carried out or administered for the well-being of
citizens individually and as a whole.

To think of these duties as being done by a weak and
whittled-down system would be fatal to this nation as a
whole and to each citizens thereof. We have politicians,
especially those in national government, who would be
appalled to have any one of these branches so weakened
that they could not carry out these functions. They cry
about all bureaucracy but their own, but that **all** want a
functioning government and know just a "little" part of it
can be cut. As it has been said, they cry "down with the
government in Washington," and then give up all else to be
a part of it. They say, in order to turn it over to the States.
One would think they would stay in the States to receive it.

Some of our experience has been with State government.

I have been in New York over sixty years and as a
citizen have worked for the betterment of communities in
the Bronx (Morrisania) and Manhattan (Harlem). I have
worked with the three levels of government and have
gotten about the same cooperation with each. The State
government has given great cooperation but under some
leadership has given the greatest "let-down" in terms of
community development. Poor judgment and the ever-
present racism can show up in any tier of government.
Cutting down on government in Washington will not
prevent the misguided government in the States.

In the "Contract" they seem to be saying that we, the
new group, are cutting down on government in
Washington; we wish to put the planning back into the

56

States <u>and in the local communities</u>. Don't you believe it! We have a supreme example in New York State of what will happen when you turn back to the State government. The great example of self-detrmination in New York State is found in the Central Harlem community which is not only the Black community that is looked on all over the world, but one which has been striving for self-determination through the years. One of the giant steps in this direction was found in the work of of the Harlem Urban Development Corporation. This corporation was founded by the Ministerial Interfaith Association (M.I.A.) of Harlem.

On the Sunday after The Reverend Martin Luther King Jr.'s assassination I, William James, of the Ministerial Association, presided over a memorial service of some 20,000 people on the Central Park Mall. The late Governor Nelson Rockefeller spoke at that service, praising the work which Dr. King had done and recounted many of his accomplishments. After the service when theGovernor was preparing to leave, he came to me and said, "We must do something to see that this work is carried on; I'll be in touch with you." I understand that the Governor attended the funeral service of Dr. King in Atlanta. He had conversations with persons there and came back to New York and later called and said the State was setting up a Board to start the Urban Development Corporation in memory of Dr. King. The Governor called our office at the M.I.A. and asked if we would organize a subsidiary of the Urban Development Corporation in Harlem as Harlem was one of the communities in which Dr. King had worked. The Governor had visited M.I.A. Now he sent H. Carl McCall the message to proceed. I was one of the founders of M.I.A. and at that time the Reverend Dr. James Gunther

57

of Transfiguration Lutheran Church was Chairman of the Board of that organization. We went out and called together a cross section of persons from the community and organized the Harlem Urban Development Corporation (HUDC). It lasted some twenty five years, giving "self help" service and developing Harlem-based development groups in Harlem.

Some of the organization's achievement are the redevelopment of 125th Street, including the designing of its physical renewal (our Chief Architect redesigned the street), building and running MART 125 for small merchants, many of whom have gone on to establish larger businesses, and renovation of the facades of most of the storefronts on 125th Street. Joining in our efforts to bring about the Adam Clayton Powell Jr. State Office Building was then Borough President of Manhattan and now Justice Constance Baker Motley and a sociologist from Maryland who obtained some 60,000 petitions to build this building when a group of pickets led by some Harlem politicians to prevent it from being a State office buidling. We worked for some twelve or more years to build an international trade center on 125th Street and Malcolm X Boulevard (Lenox Avenue), sometimes in spite of UDC. We got from the New York and New Jersey Port Authority some $50 million to be the basic grant for this facility. We were able through investment interest to add $15,000,000 for a total of $65 million. We, HUDC, with the Honorable Percy Sutton, was able to save the Apollo Theatre from being closed and took it over and aided in getting funds to renovate it with Mr. Sutton and Inner City Broadcasting Company taking over the operational program and aiding Mr. Sutton by putting in some $3 million. When it turned out that it was too small a house, seating 1400, to bring in the "big" performers as a profit-making organization, we took the property back and canceled out part of the expenditures and turned it into a non-profit public institution like Avery Fisher Hall and Carnegie Hall. We also saved the Loew's Cinema House on 125th Street in order that we may have a movie theatre in Harlem.

Housing: What can we say. We have developed some 3,000 units of housing in Harlem. It was HUDC under the leadership of Donald Cogsville who led the way for mixed income housing in Harlem when planning boards and the same public officers ridiculed us and especially Cogsville for this. Now it is the "in thing," since it has been instrumental in bringing back to Harlem large numbers of middle income families. This has cut crime and also brought back the people, and in the last years has turned Harlem's population around.

We designed and organized a section of Harlem called Bradhurst (The Bradhurst Development project). HUDC had advocated to take a low income, crime ridden area and develop it. The area chosen was from 138th Street south to 155th Street north between Bradhurst Avenue to Adam Clayton Powell Jr. Boulevard east. We are in the midst of renovating and building some 3800 units of housing, with all the social services, education, recreation, theatre facilities, businesses and all the things to make a community complete. This is to be done in five phases. The first phase is completed, the second and third are underway. This has changed the whole community. HUDC organized the churches into a group named Harlem Churches for Community Improvement (HCCI) and the Consortium for Central Harlem Development (CCHD) made up of some eleven organizations including HCCI.

William M. James

This has been one of the outstanding development in total community planning and operation.

HUDC has done more than 3000 homes and over 2000 units in brownstone façade restoration. All this was done at very little cost to landlords, families under the poverty level and families with aged persons. It also began to restore many brownstones into "condos." It aided, in the earlier stages, various churches to build houses in their communities. It has brought business activities in the community. It also put together the application and guidelines for the Empowerment Zones of the country as an aid to the Federal government's plan which had been projected by Congressman Charles Rangel, and put together the proposal for the Empowerment Zones for Harlem and Washington Heights. We planned a project, "Harlem on the Hudson," at the western end of 125th Street over the objection of one of our elected officials.

All of these things were self-help community projects, with very little of the State's money, which provided $95+ million over a 25-year period, which averages out to $4 million per year. The Division of the Budget of the State of New York year after year was saying to us that we were doing more with the limited amount of money which we are being given, more or as much as any agency in the State. We were audited annually by private and State auditors that always gave us a clean audit as to accountability.

After all of this, twenty-five years of Board members meeting monthly, giving their time for their community planning for the future of Harlem, we read one day in the press, Newsday and Crain's Magazine, that Mr. George E. Pataki, the new Governor, would be eliminating HUDC and its work folded into UDC the State organization, "located downtown". Later, through battles in the Legislature, a so-called compromise was reached that it would not be done this way. It would be given a new name with the Board appointed by Governor Pataki, with part of the Board from the community and the other part from the State, but the appointments would be done by outsiders and the power controls coming from "downtown". This is the direction we travel when we politicize everything in a partisan way. We forget about the community efforts and do things by fiat.

This new organization got a very small budget and is completely controlled by the State. The International Trade Center was eliminated and the $65 million was taken out of Harlem. The Governor did not have the good grace to speak to any of us as officials of HUDC, those who had given twenty-five years of service in organizing and development and gave thousands of hours to work in the community without compensation. He did not even answer one letter or any of our communications that were sent to him. To him, we as Black people were beneath his effort to communicate. No white newspaper printed one word of our achievements. You have at the heart of the "Contract" attitudes such as that of the Governor of New York State that will become the norm if we travel in the direction of forgetting the poor, the Blacks and others who do not have the power or know how to fight back with effectiveness. The State will control and the little people will be as serfs.

William M. James

What it Took to Break the Power that Gripped
the Nation for Some Sixty Plus Years

The bold start of Reconstruction of the nation on the race question did not stop at Black people but extended to the poor and the sick of the nation. The Great Depression changed the climate of the nation by seeing that freedom in this land meant "economic freedom" as well as freedom from bondage of the person in the body. The hunger of the body was connected with the hunger of the soul. In this world soul and body were "one unit." Therefore, the downgrading of one made the other in need. President Roosevelt's Four Freedoms brought about a new era in that thought that the poor could rise above their impoverished state and reach the heights of the upper class. It became the age for hope of the "common man" and this time women were included in this hope. There were the Blacks, the poor (unemployed) and women who had much which to look forward. Education, old age security (Social Security), the expanding of electric power throughout the land began to spread this hope. A meaningful march of progress was begun. Access by Black people to the "White House' and government councils, the placing of a woman (Frances Purkins) in the Cabinet, making jobs available through government and private industry were all a part of the beginning of this movement. Every president from Roosevelt to Nixon made some major breakthrough toward a democratic government. Truman integrated the armed forces, which had been a national disgrace—Black soldiers fighting and dying for a country in which they were separated from White soldiers by laws of the States and by practices of the armed services. Eisenhower sent Federal

63

troops to Little Rock, Arkansas and integrated the schools there that gave a lesson to the country that the States could not nullify the Constitution. He had appointed Earl Warren as Chief Justice of the United States Supreme Court, a Court that brought back the 14th Amendment of the U.S. Constitution to its real purpose for being. Eisenhower seemed to have regretted this appointment but saw it was his obligation to carry out its mandates. Kennedy sent troops into Mississippi to open the University of Mississippi to Black students and finally to protect the civil rights marchers. Johnson had already broken the "filibuster" which was the key to the Southern States preventing the United States Senate from passing laws to carry out the mandates of the 13th, 14th and 15th Amendments to the Constitution. He did this with the help of Everett McKinley Dirksen of Illinois, the Republican Minority Leader. Then, while Johnson was President, he pushed through the greatest measures for civil rights that the nation had seen since the "Reconstruction Era" which followed. Some of these were the "Voting Rights Act" and "Affirmative Action" and the "Great Society" or "War Against Poverty," which made him the President who signed more acts for the upliftment of the poor and rights for the Blacks since President Grant in the later 1860s and early '70s.

The Whole Nation was Turning to the Theme of "Basic Rights and Justice for all."

Great men and women passed through this Era and some saw this as the twilight of their careers. Some of these stalwarts were W.E.B. Dubois, James Weldon

64

Johnson, Francis J. McConnel, John Haynes Holmes, Harry Emerson Fosdick, Herbert J. Welch, Stephen A. Wise, A Philip Randolph, Marion Anderson, Mary McCleod Bethune, Mary Church Terrell, Henry Wallace, Harold Eckes, Hubert Humphrey, Wayne Morse, Eleanor Roosevelt, Walter White. There were others who were at the height of their careers such as Dorothy Height, Ann Arnold Hedgman, Percy Sutton, Thurgood Marshall, Fannie Lou Hamer, Constance Baker Motley, Nelson Rockefeller, Gloster Current, Ramsey Clark, Roy Wilkins. And there were the young movers Martin Luther King Jr., Gloria Brown, the Stokes brothers, "Jim" Lawson, Charles Rangel, Fannie Lou Hamer, John Lewis, and others. This list does not include the writers and actors who laid everything in their lives on the line. There were others who became martyrs such as Medgar Evers, Michael Swaner, James Chaney, Mr. Michael Goodman, Ms. Liazzo, James Reeb and others. There are many more in this "endless line of splendor."

These leaders and thousands more went up against an entrenched army of persons in State governments and local governments along with hundreds of policeman – the very people the Contract says should be given the funds and power to bring about a great reduction in crime. These aided wild mobs in burning buses, they turned dogs on peaceful demonstrators who had done no more than march unarmed and knelt to pray at State capitols and courthouses, praying and marching to regain their constitutional right for equality under the law. They were made criminals by people who committed criminal acts by denying them their rights through force. There was no one in the law establishment to protect them. The head of the Federal Bureau of Investigation was in conspiracy against

65

them, the State governors and legislators were in league to see that they were not granted their constitutional rights to vote, go to schools paid for from tax monies, to ride trains without being humiliated by being given a designated place, separate, as lepers of old. The State contended their constitutional right did not apply in their particular State. They had to live, travel and breathe in these States which were in common league against them.

Now the "Contract With America," penned and signed by many of the Republicans in the House of Representatives – which is supposed to legislate for the "good and welfare" for all the people – is now working to turn back the clock to the place where the States will have the right to take away many of these individual rights so valiantly fought for by so many now living and dead.

Let us Look at Some of the Struggle

The struggle for American democracy in the United States of America.

"Will There Be Turning Back"

> "The influence from the American Creed thus had, and still had, a double-direction. On the one hand, the equalitarian creed operates directly to suppress the dogma of the Negro's racial inferiority and to make peoples thoughts more independent of race, creed, or color" as the American slogan runs.

On the other hand, it indirectly calls forth the same dogma to justify a blatant exception to the creed."[8]

This was said in 1944, as the book "An American Dilemma" was published. In the South, "strict segregation" reigned supreme. The Supreme Court was beginning to give decisions favorable to the inclusion of Black people, the Roosevelt Administration had laid the groundwork for basic economic and social change in the whole society. Then later in the next decade came the monumental Supreme Court decision that declared that "Separate was inherently unequal" and asked for the integration of schools throughout the land. This not only affected the schools but the whole society in ways that it moved and breathed. This threw the 13th, 14th and 15th Amendments back on the table and back in the Courts. These Amendments were designed specifically for the Black people after slavery but was a pillar for guaranteed rights of all "groups" as they spelled out a new push for liberation among the Black and other peoples. This aroused once again the hopes and aspirations, especially for Black people. Through organizations like the NAACP and The Urban League, which had worked faithfully for such change, a new awareness of their possibilities in this country came to Black people. Some began to take new starts Connecting Reconstruction with the Fifties and Sixties of our time.

There arise a strange opposition in the nation by an especially large number of white males to tear down the walls of "law and order" and go back to "lynch law" through such groups as "The White Citizens Council," The

---

[8] Gunnar Myrdal, "An American Dilemma," p. 89.

William M. James

Association for the Advancement of White People," and others. On the political scene the talk of the far right was of "nullification," meaning to ignore the Supreme Court and, in fact, the Constitution. "State Rights" groups began to cry for placing things back in the hands of the State Governments. This was as it was before the Civil War. But there was a strong reaction from the liberal forces joining with the Black organizations. Out of this came "The Congress of Racial Equality (CORE), the Student Non-Violent Coordinating Committee and the powerfully well thought out Southern Christian Leadership Conference under the leadership of Dr. Martin Luther King Jr. All of these movements were "non-violent" but with an aggressive civil disobedience philosophy springing from historical persons such as Henry David Thoreau, a New England abolitionist, Mahatma Gandhi, and back to Jesus Christ who kept a steady course for truth and right in spite of society.

There was the violence of the rightist segregationist. Many lives were lost in the struggle but the end goals were looked at beyond the suffering. Dr. King had studied first under Dr. Walter Rosenbush and then under Dr. Allan Knight Chalmers, and Dr. Harold DeWolf of Boston University. All were steeped in the idea of justice. Dr. Chalmers had been the Treasurer of the movement that entered the famous "Scottsboro Case," a case where nine Black young men and boys were tried and convicted in a case that said they had raped two white women near Scottsboro, Alabama. These were all a group fo "hobos' but the case became the watershed of civil rights in court. One of the young women finally turned and became a defense witness, and said this did not happen. But the main result of the case was that the lower courts were overturned by the Supreme Court several times because it said that the young men had not been tried by a jury of their peers, meaning there were no Blacks on the jury for Blacks were completely banned from the jury selection process by the State of Alabama and most or all Southern states. This was deliberately and intentionally done in violation of the 14th Amendment of the Constitution.

The Civil Rights Movement in the 1960s brought about the greatest coalition for "civil liberties" that the nation has ever seen. But the decent amongst the "States" were very strong. It took strong action from the then Attorney General Robert Kennedy to move the FBI to act when violence on the non-violent was investigated.

J. Edgar Hoover, who was head of the Federal Bureau of Investigation, busied himself in seeing that Dr. King was spied on continually. It was Governor Wallace of Alabama who "stood in the school house door" to prevent students from entering the University of Alabama. He lived to change his mind in the year 1995, in connection with the anniversary of the March in Selma. He was rolled in a wheelchair to demonstrate how right the earlier marches were and to repent of his previous stand against them. It was a wonderful sight to see the former Governor Wallace, the prime symbol of racial separation and discrimination shaking hands with my friend Rev. Dr. Joe Lowery, the President of SCLC. One thought what great things God can do in human relations.

Governor Orville Forbus of Arkansas sent out the State guard to prevent Black students from entering the Little Rock High School. It was a "middle of the roader," President Dwight D. Eisenhower who concluded that the Constitution as interpreted by the Supreme Court could not be defied or nullified by the State Executive or the State

69

Government and he sent the U.S. troops to guarantee the rights of these students in Arkansas. One of the students who the U.S. government guaranteed these rights to enter that school is Ernest Green who became a great man in our time. He was in the Department of Labor in the Carter Administration and now works in the famous brokerage company Shearson Lehman Hutton of the American Express Corporation. As I have said, it has been the U.S. Government which has been much more vigilant than any of the States in protection of individual rights.

It may not have been on the surface of the argument but its roots are the same as is found in the "American Dilemma" in the "Nineteen Forties" and the same basic dangers of racial thinking that was a carry over from the Eighteen Nineties which crushed the concept of the American dream as seen in the Declaration of Independence and was kept out of the Constitution on account of slavery of the Black people. The slave owners of the South overruled Jefferson, Wyatt and Franklin, who had a clause in the draft of the Declaration condemning King George for the salve trade. The clashes of ideas over and against the reality of the non-acceptance of equality of the so-called "races" was the cause of a deep cleavage in our nation. This was shown in the Korner Report (named for the Governor of Illinois who headed a commission to study the effect of the racial divisions in the nation in our recent time) which showed this division was widening but did not see a solution on the future horizon. From the Roosevelt era through the Carter Administration there were great changes that came about by law. In this atmosphere, the Black people began to advance economically and in the social spectrum. There seemed to be a "way out"—the coalition of Black civil rights groups, the effects on the legal position of Blacks, the accentuation of education, the opening of the large universities North and South to Blacks. It seemed as the movement was toward the upward level for Blacks in the United States. The State courts, and the opening of the political ballot boxes and the push for better jobs and education in the political process seemed to make it so. With the assassination of Dr. King and the Kennedy brothers and the demonstrations, and the deterrence during the Vietnam War shocked the nation and blunted the Civil Rights Movement. There were national changes. This turned the nation toward another agenda. The Johnson Administration which had laid so much of the groundwork for the Civil Rights Movement was now in trouble with other problems, such as the Vietnam War.

The Rise of the Black Nationalist.

There began to be riots in some of our major cities. There were both sincere beliefs that "Black Power" with the clenched fist was the answer to the American dilemma. There was a Black Nationalism on the other hand that was grounded in the possibility of separation of Whites and Blacks. This had come from some Black groups imitating such White groups as the KKK, only reversing the inferiority theory and laying it at the door of the "White Man." This divided the Black people, some holding to the non-violent and integration of a society where "Black and White together" was the solution. While other were for putting 'Whites" out of all Black Movements and organizations, the fight for separate dormitories and other separate facilities. All coalitions began to break apart. The whole movement toward the liberal Whites and the progressive Blacks began to fade. The leadership of the Black Movement began to shift from the Church to the Black politicians many were more individualistic in their leadership.

The one factor that had been the crown jewel of Black progress in all of this was the <u>Church</u>, not necessarily the "Black Church" alone but a coalition of Black, White and other religious leaders. Some of the great leaders in these movements were the United Church of Christ, the United Methodist Church, especially the women's group, and in the church the connection between other Black and White liberals had begun to fade. The rise of women clergy, begun by the Methodist Church's General Conference in 1956 and followed by the other major Protestant denominations and in later years it was thought this would bring a more progressive push in the church – a more favorable attitude toward the Black Christian but it seemed to have had the opposite effect. In the past, the church through the women was pushing for a fair deal, not only for themselves but for a "fair deal' for all. When they rose as clergy-theologians, they began to push for women's rights and many times failed to make coalitions with the Blacks especially the Black males. Therefore, the liberal push of the Thelma Stevenses from Mississippi, the M.E. Tillys of Atlanta and many others began to be lost.

The failing of the coalitions of liberals and the rise of the Black Nationalist's Separatist Movement gave opportunity for the rise of the Conservative "Religious Right' to have free reign. The middle of the road White began to be the "to the right of the road" White Males. The "New Rich" Whites from oil, the real estate magnates, and later the entertainment and casino magnates were neither philanthropic or altruistic. Many were not religious at all.

The liberal began to be boldly attached, it became almost as bad to be called a liberal in our present times as it was to be called "nigger lover" during the 1890s. Even one our presidential candidates, and who was vice president, said of the opposition, "He's a card-carrying liberal, he is a member of the American Civil Liberties Union." This caused us to have almost a "not contest, no challenge" government.

William M. James

When Democrats Became Republicans They Did Not Have to Switch Ideology.

The Civil Rights Movement and the Voter Rights Act caused the development of a coalition of Blacks and Whites in the South to form political coalitions. Both attitudes and political ideas began to make rapid changes. When the Democrats in the South had been "conservative rightist" in the segregationist South where race was concerned. Now they found it necessary to form some kind of accommodation and voting coalition with the Blacks. This was true more so in the Black Belts like parts of Mississippi, Alabama, Georgia, Louisiana, South Carolina, Western Tennessee and parts of Texas. This accommodation along with school integration drove large blocks of Whites to the Republican Party. This again, as Dr. Myrdal states, was because there was the "racist" stance rather than party label that caused them to move over, thus, as before, race became a major factor in the political party role.

The movement in the South affected the political scene of the whole nation. The Republican political gains in the South which had their seed sown by the Nixon Administration which was anti-Black but more subtly so than the Republican Administrations that followed, as we have stated. The riots in the predominantly Black community helped crystallize the country in crushing the liberal movement. The cry of persons such as Rap Brown saying "Burn, baby, burn" sent a reaction wave across the nation that helped the "Radical Right" to recoup their losses from the ugly scene of the "Bull O'Connor" dogs and the 1968 scenes of the clubbing of the marchers, the

75

turning on of the high-powered water hoses on the students in South Carolina. The murders of the civil rights persons in Mississippi and Alabama, the blowing up of the church in Alabama and killing of small children at worship. The burning o Black churches in other places in the South. The entire nation recoiled from these violent acts against a non-violent movement. The nation acted and brought about some positive changes.

Later it was doubtful if all of the riots brought about in Black communities were spontaneous actions. There are the lingering questions, was this a conspiracy to kill the civil rights movement and the gains which it was making in singing, ""Black and White together, we shall not be moved"? Were there many forces in our society to cause the riots? Was it strange that after the presidential election of Nixon the riots ceased? Why did some of the Black nationalists retire, well healed financially at a very young age after Nixon's election?

One group or nation had the power to wipe out another group or nation – genocide.

The history of slavery as we recently saw it was a history that brought racism to be in the conscious and subconscious of American life. This puts persons of African descent, United States Blacks, and the other African descendants, Puerto Ricans, Cubans, South and Central Americans and those from other Caribbean islands and from all over the world in another category from Black citizen the U.S.A. The most pointed disadvantaged ones are the Blacks of the U.S.A. They have a deep stigma against them. This stigma is so pronounced that other African descendants, such as the Hispanic-speaking with Black ancestors, seem to avoid this association in order that they will not be classified with the United States Blacks.

76

This comes truer with people of color from Asia, especially the Japanese many of whom do not want to be identified with people of color who are U.S. Blacks because of the stigma this might place on them in their relationship with White America. Through interaction with Black Americans, this could give the Hispanics and Asians a distinct political advantage in the long run because the numbers of these three groups would put each other on a political level with the Whites, especially where the dominate White male is concerned. This is one of the reasons that the dominate White male group will play down the possibility of such coalitions.

They will plant seeds of dissension and separation among Blacks, Hispanics and Asians to play down each other. This is a planned and planted psychology to keep these groups from joining politically. This method can be found in all institutions.

The Church and Its Role in Both the Inegrationist and Separatist Movements

The Christian Church formed a divided front in the Negro question. The impact of the European class system coming out of the middle ages has had a great effect on the church and the race system. Just as England suppressed the colonies and held them subservient, so did the colonies suppress their citizens on different levels of social strata. In the days of indentured servitude and the suppression of Native Americans (Indians), Blacks were looked to be in about the same category but then as the Whites worked their way out of indentured servanthood and the Native Americans were forcibly moved from their land, Blacks began to be pushed down to a lower level. One of the reasons, Blacks were more easily identifiable than these two other groups. Another was that slavery was beginning to take on a permanency.

In various churches these factors took on different forms. When the "American Revolution" came and independence began to be equated with freedom, the church began to be a main factor in its theology and ideology. Myrdal states, in the American Dilemma, "The ideas of the American Revolution added their influence to these of some early Christian thinkers and preachers, particularly among the Quakers, in deprecating these arguments (that was that the biological difference made the Negro naturally unequal, an outcast among Peoples) – but many believed that human beings natural rights merged with the Golden Rule in Christianity, "Do unto others, as you would have them go unto you".[9]

Myrdal goes on to quote Jefferson in his autobiography in 1821.

> "...It was found that they would not bear the proposition [gradual emancipation] nor will it bear it even this day. Yet the day is not far distant when it must bear it, or worse will follow. Nothing is more certainly written in the book of fate than that these people are to be free." (Jefferson's Autobiography).

It was among Washington's first wishes, "to see a plan adopted for the abolition of it [slavery] but there is only one proper and effectual mode by which it can be

---

[9] An American Dilemma, Vol 1., p. 85.

accomplished, and that is by legislative authority." In this period the main American religious denominations also went on record as condemning slavery.

In the Twentieth century, there arose in this country many forward looking thinking liberal ministers, both in the White and Black churches. This placed the churches and the body politic in harmony and the liberal wing of the church joined hands to fight the social battles for the "underclasss." These were the ordinary laborers. The labor movement became the target of the Conservative Right. The religionist of the Right did not enter the political arena in full force at that time as did the liberals. This was a strange combination, for the active religious liberals were many times liberal in social matters, especially the "Negro question," and conservatives in finance and fiscal matters.

The weight of the labor organizations began to shift voting power toward liberalism, especially in the big cities. Though the labor organization would eventually become a boost to the Black movement, at first they allied with the segregationists and as far as possible denied the Blacks membership in the labor organization. The forming of the Sleeping Car Union, under the leadership of A. Philip Randolph, became the political center of Blacks in the labor movement, the American Federation of Labor. The CIO under the Ruther Brothers, good Lutherans, and the coal miners under John L. Lewis fought for inclusiveness. A Philip Randolph was the "Father of Negro Mass Protest." It was he who planned one March on Washington and got a partial "loaf" from the Roosevelt Administration, but it was also he that planned the March on Washington that gave Martin Luther King Jr. immortality with his "I Have A Dream" speech.

In the meantime, earlier in the century, the National Council of Churches was being formed that joined together the forces of the Protestant and Eastern Orthodox Churches that gave voice to liberalism from a religious point of view.

These two forces, labor and the liberal wing of the churches had been given great allies in political fields. Such men of history as Theodore Roosevelt, Woodrow Wilson (who was not in the Black man's corner), Senator Robert J. La Follite and Justice Louis D. Brandeis. Brandeis came up against the giants of laissez faire capitalism and won many cases against the giants of that age. He was for the "entire' public process. Despite his liberal views he was confirmed as Justice of the Supreme Court and became one of the most outstanding Justices in history.

Then came the Roosevelt Administration; at this time the church was flourishing. This was helping the progressive movement. Jobs were being produced, in that the thousands of unemployed could be gainfully employed. Public housing was being built to accommodate the poor. There was no public housing before. Savings became secure in banks. Educational opportunities were broadened through the N.Y.A. for education, old age financing through Social Security Insurance. The so-called races were beginning to work together with social institutions and government help. A great step was made in both the national student loan program and the student grant program sponsored by Senator Pell of Rhode Island. The Roosevelt Administration through the demands of the society was not stopped because in saving the nation in the Great Depression he saved the rich and poor alike. The national government acts began to be the real guardian of rights of all people. Just as the "Contract" is projective now, the "rightist conservatives" of that time were promoting the same as the "Contract" promises now and predicting doom of the nation if the progress was not stopped.

William M. James

The Supremacy of Laissez Faire Capitalism – An Economic Doctrine which Opposes Governmental Regulations in the Economic System

"Leave us alone. The big corporations will police themselves. What about the people? What about the people? Will we know what's better for them! Let industry alone, they will regulate themselves."

This was the stance that brought about the Great Depression which was the very cause of BIG government to have to protect the people from Big Industry. It was the Federal government that saved the nation from economic collapse and in so doing saved industry to serve the nation. As free industry with representative government the arm of the people, to serve as referee in the economic game of life where the stakes are so high.

There are certain safety nets built into the system which have prevented economic collapse in a nation fast-growing both in population and technology. Some of these nets have served us well as "entitlements" such as Society Security, bank insurance, now Medicare and others in Education and Research of various kinds as the need for both individual and national security. The "Contract" would pluck the safety net from under the working poor and other poor.

The "Contract" states their priority in saying, the first and foremost priority of the Federal government is "national defense." Some individuals go further in saying that the Federal government should stay out of most other things in our society. This might have been possible when

83

the nation was made up as an agrarian society. But this is not true in our age. The very complexity that brought about excessive military spending connected with the large industrial complexes that reap the financial benefits from this process makes it more difficult to control.

There must be a national control over both in order that the national government can be the final mediator between the two. It was this marriage, the marriage between the military and the industrial complexes that the late President Dwight Eisenhower warned this nation against. He saw the dire consequence of such unregulated complexes.

Some years ago we were having the massive "anti-nuke" demonstrations. One of the staged held was in New York. By fate I, William James, became President of the cooperative that put on the June 12th Rally in New York City. We heard loud warnings from various of the many organizations involved. The warning to the then present situation that while we in this country and Russia were putting our interests and economics in the nuclear weapons race, Japan and Germany were producing usable goods. Wanting to gain markets in the usable technical fields, so they predicted that this would affect our economy for years to come. This would affect our economy at the top and it would leave us with a shortfall for years to come. Therefore, it is not our giving to "welfare" or social programs that has brought about our large deficits and interest payments but it has been the paying for past and present wars. Also for future wars which <u>must not come</u>. It was not illegal or legal aliens on which we spend which has caused our huge national debts but the great cost of maintaining and projecting the military. Therefore, the "Contract's" emphasis on a "strong defense" is hallow indeed, if we decay morally and ethically from inside the union. The Reagan Administration cut taxes and raised military spending. This made the U.S. debt soar and interest rates became fearful.

There is a great irony and a great danger in the "Contract's" position, in that they say on one hand that they are for safe streets, they content that the crime bill is greatly flawed because it had in it thirty billion dollars over six years including five and four-tenths billion for prevention programs and seven and nine-tenths billion for new prisons, and eight tenths billion for new police officers. On the other hand, the "Contract" takes the position that the way to deal with crime is make laws with harsher "punishment"— the loss of the idea of redeemability of the wrongdoer in society would cure crime. The "reform" solution is not really reform but reverting back to a former age.

The "Contract" does not take into consideration that the "government" can become one of the "government against the people."

One of the great things that the government has going for it is the idea of freedom built into the Constitution—one of the fundamentals of our freedom, should not be changed to "get at the so-called criminal types." The danger is that when it is opened up for one purpose we might be building a state that will trample freedom underfoot. The entrance for the State to dominate the individual is to let the State or constabulary have free reign, to be judge and jury over peoples' homes and person. There is grave danger in letting the policeman make the judgment on search and seizures without court action. Those who have lived under the rule of police, constable and lynch men can testify to the fact that such terror of the homes starts out as a measure to get at a "particular type" of menace to society, then the constabulary begins to determine who is the menace to

85

society. The Constitution is not to be amended to limit peoples' lives or try to force people to be morally upright.

I happen to live in a police precinct (the 30th in New York City) where numerous charges have been made against police corruption. You will find some of the same in any city in our country. The majority of the policemen are fine people, but the laws and rules must be weighed toward freedom of the individual. Let us see that the 14th Amendment stand and the exclusionary rule remain as a reminder to all, that a person cannot be convicted by evidence that is illegally obtained.

Let Us Take a Look at Where We have Been and Meditate in Our Own Deep Thought on Where We Ought to Go.

Our forefathers and the Creator of history have given a past on which one can use the guidelines and the foundations already laid to build a world like "Paradise." We have the God given material substance and it has been shown through the Revelations from God the way to spiritual excellence to fit us to live in a new order—"a Paradise-world." We as Christians pray "Thy Kingdom come, they will be done on earth as it is in Heaven." Others say it in their own way. But all can hear the tonal sound of Thomas Jefferson as he says, "We hold these truths to be self evident, that all persons are created equal – and endowed by t he Creator with certain inalienable rights, among these are life, liberty and [the opportunity for] the pursuit of happiness." This is one of the "way stations" that we stop to read on our way to the New World—where God's will is done on earth as like heaven. Let us not pass it by as a nation or as an individual without stopping (not pausing) but stopping and reading and fully digesting its present effect and its long range implication. If each person and nation will heed this saying and from whence it comes, and who is beyond the pen of Jefferson, we will be on our way to this "New World, the one like Paradise by hearing the voices of our forefathers who knew that Jesus loved the poor and the right.

We stand in danger that while we read, new voices will call with compelling sounds and cunning propaganda telling you that they can offer you, an America, a Contract that will give you a future much more grandiose in its results than that which was given of old. They will say that there are truths in this Contract, one that will let you have payless years in taxes. They will say that your taxes are supporting the lazy, those of loose morals, children that should not be in the world in the first place, the foreigners and their children. You can keep all this for yourselves. They will tell you, great debts have been piled up in your attempt to aid the poor, take care of the needy, the aged needing health care, places to live being subsidized for the poor. They will try to divert your eyes from the words, "We hold these truths to be axiomatic that all <u>persons however</u> or wherever born in what estate they came are created equal and endowed by <u>"their Creator</u>." They will throw a sign before your eyes saying, "Sign our Contract; we have the answer," even better than those liberals like Jefferson. But these will still stand through the sands of time – <u>By their Creator, Life, liberty</u>. There will be one who stands beside the reading holding another sign from ancient times. It will read, "Thus saith the Lord, for three transgressions – ya for four, I will not turn away the punishment thereof, because they sold the righteous for silver, and the poor for a pair of shoes; that pant after the dust of the earth, on heads of the poor and turn aside the way of the meek." Amos 2:6

The noise might sound louder about taxes, welfare and keeping your money. And then another stands by the reading. This one looks as if he comes from "paradise." This sign reads, "The spirit of the Lord is upon me because he hath anointed me to bring 'good news' to the poor, he has sent me to heal the broken hearted, to bring deliverance to the captives" Luke 4:18, (to bring out the prisoner from the prison house {from Isaiah}}. He also had another sign that said, "When the son of man shall come unto his glory, and all the holy angels with him, then he sall sit upon the throne of his glory. And before him gathered all nations and he shall separate them from one another; and he shall say to them on his right hand, 'come ye blessed of my father, inherit the kingdom prepared for you from the foundation of the world, for I was hungry and you fed me, I was thirsty and you gave me drink, a stranger (out of doors) and you took me in, naked and you clothed me, in prison and you came to me...'" Matthew 25:31-36.

The signs that point to a New World will have many other signs pointing the way to the paths which we must follow and the way and people with whom we must be reconciled.

It is not enough to say that we are endowed by the Creator but we must come to understand what the Creator is calling on us to do to build that "bridge to the future."

We must not be duped by those who would offer a road of non-sacrifice to build the best society. We all must we willing to give of ourself and our substances.

The "Contract" seems to say that we must have a non-sacrificial or non-caring society, and still build that New World. We must understand that we will have the weak with us. We must be prepared to help them. We must not exchange the covenant of God or his <u>Sure</u> Contract with us for a "Contract" with society "as we know it." We will find that God's covenant is more practical. His creation is the most practical thing that has ever been imagined.

The rest of this paper reviews from whence we have come, some of the pitfalls which we have gone around. We hope that we have learned from recent history how to go forward and not go back into the social paths of the past.

We number among those visionaries a host of patriots along with those who look beyond the horizons at other people inhabiting other lands but seeing them all as a part of that mighty host which we call humanity. The dreamer, no more than that these prophets, projectors, and sayers of the future which they in their time toiled with body and soul, or mind, to make sure that their predictions would some day come to full fruition. In this "endless line of splendor" we find Jesus and a host of martyrs who believe so deeply in all of the children of God's creation was of infinite worth that gave their lives in order that this concept would live and grow. Then we have those who articulated this to be made as the foundation of what they found to be an eternal truth. This was penned by Thomas Jefferson as he wrote, "We hold these truths to be self-evident that <u>all</u> <u>men</u> (meaning persons) are created equal and endowed by the Creator with certain unalienable rights (which cannot be separated from the person so endowed), among these are life, liberty and the pursuit of happiness." Then in the great struggle to bring this nation into oneness over being a series of States claiming this one thing, Abraham Lincoln spoke these words, "Four score and seven years ago our forefathers brought forth on this continent a new nation conceived in liberty and dedicated to the proposition that all men are created equal. Now we are engaged in a great civil war testing whether this nation or <u>any</u> nation so conceived and so dedicated can long endure." When the war ended so many thought: Now this is done, the victory is ours, the test is positive, all men shall be free. But with the bold start from a slave holding society and a society holding a pro-slave bias the battle was to range on even until now. The bold start of freedom was halted by methods of force and chicanery and by seemingly good intentioned propaganda. In the 1890's all the equality lines failed to get around the Constitution by nullification and the Supreme Court gave a ruling, "separate and equal," really legalizing what we later called in South Africa, "Apartheid." I use this word to bring home the situation that held from the 1890's to the 1960's and 1970's in this country. The Courts permitted the proposition that the States administered the "Apartheid" laws. The "State Righter" had won, and the truth of "equality" of mankind was lost. As far as the 13th, 14th and 15th Amendments, they had been nullified for all practical purposes.

The fight for equality had to start all over again. There rose the Niagara Movement which culminated in the N.A.A.C.P., a group of different ethnic and religious backgrounds who vowed to carry on the fight. There were the courageous martyrs again. The resistance to regaining freedom took its toll because the "States Rights groups" were in control. They had the "right" to lynch, maim, mutilate and burn without fear of reprisal from the State or the suppressed people. There were continuing voices of protest and a continuing clamor for equity that one word, freedom, kept ringing. The "States Righters" controlled part of the House of Representatives with the Senate standing ready to filibuster any remedial legislation. There came about a Court that began to go back behind the "separate and equal States Rights Court" and began to look at the real situation. Thus the Warren Court, the Wearing Court, the Vincent Court began to make a difference. They reverted to the Constitution and individual rights. They began to switch the"States Rights" containing the Blacks back on the human or individual rights track, guaranteed in the Constitutional rights (Federally enforced).

William M. James

The Grave Problem with "States Rights"

The "States Rights" argument has come down from colonial days. The central question was, how could the people, mostly land owning gentry, form a government that would include "rankless" and common laboring masses to have full participation? Then later it became clear that you have a multiplicity of factors that Mother England and many other European countries had imported to us but did not have themselves. Some of these were: the Black Africans' growing population of both free men and slaves; the immigration of Asians and other groups; the Native American (so-called Indian) population who were already established here; and above all, we were creating a new type of society in which individual liberty was the basic doctrine. How would this egalitarianism hold in a society that was being put together by a gentry which was holding to an Anglo-European model of a class structured society? This became the dilemma of the founding fathers. Jefferson, Franklin, Marshall (who became Chief Justice), Hamilton and others had the idea that the English model had to be abandoned because the colonial system was one of tyranny from which the colonies in America had suffered. This had brought on the Revolution. But there were the "Southern Gentry" who had fears of losing their privileged places in society by the rise of the"free market" and the working class or common laborers in the North and the other highest priority was to hold to slavery of the Blacks in the South. This became a part of their economic, social and religious life that the "male gentry" would keep their status. On the other hand there was a rising type that was moving toward this democratic individualistic egalitarianism which made the common man its peer and would give the slave the same rights under <u>Natural Law</u> as the master. Jefferson became President and in his lifetime had two of his proteges follow as President. They were Madison and Monroe. This tipped the scales toward a Peoples democracy but did not kill the resistance. The free labor question and the abolition question kept growing.

Then there arose the great champion of "States Rights" that was to carry the fight into the first part of the nineteenth Century. His name was John C. Calhoun of South Carolina. His argument, many times illogical and impractical but persistent. He even argued for a federation with two Presidents. His argument was that sovereign rights of any system should not rest on the rights of the individual but on the individual rights as the States would grant them.

The one place where Calhoun was rebuffed by even his common friends was on the question of "nullification." When the states did not agree with the federal Constitution, Eugene Genovese in his book, The <u>Southern Tradition</u>, says "Calhoun failed to convince any Southern state except South Carolina of the constitutionality of nullification, even the South Carolinians were seriously divided." This held the South which was at first deeply divided on States Rights, especially where slavery was concerned. Then came the Missouri Compromise in 1820 by Henry Clay of Kentucky. This also made Daniel Webster of New England from this time forward a fixture in American debate. Then the Compromise of 1850 led by Henry Clay and opposed by his cousin Cassius Clay, a Kentucky anti-slave Clay, from whom the great boxer, Cassius Clay now Mohammed Ali, got his name. Then in 1858 came to the forefront a commoner, Abraham Lincoln, who believed in the egalitarian rights over the "States Rights." He seemed to have defeated himself while running for the U.S. Senate against Steven A. Douglas by his greatest speech, in which he quoted Jesus when he said, "A house divided against itself cannot stand." Then he added, we must be "all slave or all free." This is said to have doomed his prospect for election to the Senate. Douglas won.

But by fate or universal design Lincoln was elected to the presidency in 1860 and was to preside over the remaking of the federal Constitution, the arbiter of slavery and the adjudicator of freedom and liberty. A thing in society is never settled for all times; therefore, John C. Calhoun as the now new conservative rightist Republican and some conservative Democrats argue that the States can do more in granting freedom than the federal Constitution, that the governors of the States who are elected by the people of the several States can do more in unifying the nation in a total interest than all the people electing the President and the Congress to represent all the States together. States Rights has always been a danger to minority groups such as Blacks, Asians, Hispanics. Various States left alone have and will discriminate in educational appropriations, jobs and union regulations, the distribution of money for health in inner city slums. All pay money in taxes and since we claim to be since the Civil War, one nation under God that we as the one nation would have one formula for distribution of all of these dollars and resources as goods that would be distributed by a just formula for all in the same category and under the same conditions.

We stand at a critical time in history to see whether the rightist "States Rights" movement will take us back to the political battles which we believed had been won in the fight over the framing of the Constitution and its safeguards in the egalitarian battles giving rights to the individual. Now we stand to go back to fight again over whether we will have government "by the people" as a direct representative democracy through the direct vote of all the people or will we have the "land owning gentry" of the Middle Ages have the States to fix our rights as individual rights by their power in regions of State where more prejudices exist – the States. This is more crucial than it looks on the surface. What are the hidden agendas or what mischief will this process bring about?

We will not see our direction clearly until we see that it is "States Rights" versus "Individual Rights." And States Rights vs the federal government. States Rights differ markedly from the rights for the individual as states in the human rights amendments of the Constitution. Again, Genovese points this out in his book, <u>Southern Tradition</u>, that "The conservatives have struggled with a problem that resists solution." He says, "The logic of their political philosophy and constitutional principles leads to programs to limit government interference in civil society to a bare minimum. The logic of their commitment to the defense of what are now loosely called "traditional values" in a society in which the market dominates not only the economy but the society itself compels them to consider government interference as the only feasible way to sustain a society in which those values can survive."[10]

The "Contract" is moving toward an unenviable position of government not interfering with social conditions but shall only interfere with those "<u>they</u>" think government should, such as abortions, personal behavioral matters and the like. "Let the industrial complexes deal

---

[10] "Southern Tradition," p. 74.

with job solution, other matters that affect economics, and those things having to do with the industrial complex regulate themselves." "We will regulate how many times the people can elect a person to office, how judges should sentence criminals but people's insurance and health care must be regulated by these companies." This is simplistic – but it gives a clue to the general dangerous trend.

We have quoted "An American Dilemma" as a definitive study in depth that "racial" thinking and action which have affected most sections of our society. Sometimes this is done overtly, and sometimes covertly, sometimes consciously and sometimes subconsciously, but most times this factor is present. Though "race" is not boldly stated in the "Contract," it is generally present. Genovese again says, "Southern conservatives today know that the old South's determination to limit the power of the national government corresponds closely to the social reality of a slave society in which maximum authority had to be placed in the hands of masters under conditions of strict social stratification. They also know that the assertion of political rights of the individual did not always mesh well with the corporate tendencies and holding of slaves as property." Thomas Roderick Dew, with special clarity, had seen the tension between those tendencies and the principles of the liberal bourgeois theory much admired reflecting the lessons of Greek history. He issued the stern warning, "Governments of antiquity, no matter of what kind, were considered possessed of every power. There were no constitutions limiting their authority, no rights reserved for individuals. The state was everything, the individual only became important through the state. The government might be the most complete despot on earth, but if each one has his equal share in that despotism, then he had liberty. The danger in extremes is when they entrap us, they do it without logic but make their own logic to fit their own theory."

We stand in grave danger because we have not taught the true meaning of liberty to this United States generation. Therefore, one has to grope to find a "ground" for his/her actions. So many do not have a solid "point of view" of what government should be, because they have not been taught the true basics that brought this nation about. Therefore, when we talk of "States Rights" vs individual rights they do not see the difference. Many do not participate in the election process by voting because we do not see that this is a great way to open society in order that we can have the great say through this process. We are like persons who do not appreciate "fresh" air until they suffocate with staleness.

The "Contract" with America" is not a document or concept arrived at through deep and prayerful thought with a goal of justice and just treatment for all. But it is deeply a thorough writing for political purposes and it is in some places false propaganda in order that many of the false beliefs of people may be perpetuated. One of these is that the police on the local scene can be better in dealing with criminals or with preventing crime, than the social institutions of a community such as the churches, community centers, supervised recreational facilities (even midnight basketball). These assertions do not take into consideration the varied types of police which our nation has. This breaks down the community's faith in government when in many of the ghettos what is seen is police graft, the ignoring of crime, brutality, sometimes the foulest mouths on the streets. From this, many youngsters take their cue and become bitter against government in general. There are many policemen who are kind, gentlemen-like, and try to carry out their duties in a civil way. But many are not gentlemen of the force.

I just finished being the advisor to a person who earned a doctorate degree. What a fine piece of work was her dissertation. But she had worked for years as an advocate for women in the criminal justice systems of New York. Sometimes one almost went to tears when reading the first hand experience and widespread research in the paper. Then when I came back and read the "Contract," I wondered: Are these writers "for real" or are they people who do not know the "real" situations? Or have they ever studies or known first hand, as I have, prisons where persons are treated as human beings and given hope? While there, how hostility is reduced. This, over and against the punishment theory, which has much increased in out time.

The "Contract" is going to provide tax credits to cure all ills of our society – tax credits for adoptions, tax credits for financial profit, gain for caring for the aged by creating tax credits, but there are many needs that have no money to pay for these things to get tax credit. Family values are things and concepts that cannot be legislated. The greatest way that Congress could help family values is by becoming living examples of great family life in their own families and not propagandizing and passing laws that will regulate families by trying to make them morally correct by cutting off their funds. The Congress could help by seeing that food and medical supplies, water supplies are kept pure and uncontaminated and that price gouging does not take advantage of the public.

This nation has been one of great achievement. Its greatest pitfall has come from its racism and group-ism.

Much of this has come from politicians latching on to some of the basic prejudices that are overt actions and exploiting them for political gain. This is found in too many politicians across all the ethnic lines. Therefore, it behooves us all to stop our subtle ways and codes of divisiveness. When the poor are pitted against the rich and the middle people against the others, it becomes a sad thing to see. This "Contract" is divisive, in that it places some people such as prisoners in a fixed position. They become a class which cannot be helped according to the "Contract." It seems to be saying that young mothers are getting babies just to get on welfare. It would be a just process to try to see why are more teenagers having babies than to conclude the reason just by looking for "Aid to Dependent Children." We all might be able to reach conclusions that might aid in having plans for begetting children. If these could have walked the streets of New York with me over the last forty plus years and seen the numbers of hundreds of young people who had been incarcerated, some drug addicts – stealing anything they could find, street gangsters fighting, anti-social to the core. I would hear the testimony of these now, since redeemed and educated, some businessman, professionals of all types, clergy, in great standing. More than 1,000 of them would write the "Contract" and say that all should take this way out for our society and we in a massive way can rehabilitate a drug and crime-ridden society

We have tried in this writing to look at a basic philosophy and theology that has come to us through the ages of how God and society have differed in the planning of a society.

Since the "Contract" seemed to be a completely secular and a materialistic document dependent on laws, deregulations, money spending and withholding, it seems to say that the cure of the ills of our society will depend on the budget balancing. I would suggest that we all reflect on some deeper things that we might do. First, to see that money will not cure our ills. We need to rethink that great document, the Declaration of Independence, "We hold these truths to be self evident, that all men (persons) are created equal and endowed by the Creator with certain inalienable rights, among these are life, liberty and the pursuit of happiness."

With this we should rethink the saying of Franking D. Roosevelt when we have the four freedoms, two of which we wish were embraced in the "Contract." They are, freedom from <u>want</u> and freedom from <u>fear</u>.

Then let us hear the words of Jesus as he said, "The spirit of the Lord is upon me for he had anointed me to preach (bring) the "good news" to the poor. To set at liberty the captive, bring out the prisoner from the prison house," Then he said, "When I was hungry you fed me, naked you clothed me, out of doors you took me in."

Which we will follow, the "Contract with America" or the Covenant with God? As for me, I will hold to the "Covenant."

A Ray of Hope

In believing in God and trusting his "Holy Word", many strange things have happened and can point to the future. We are able to look back at some of the impossibilities of the past that have made us have a valid presence.

In this presence, we see things that will give us a "Ray of Hope" for the future. We conclude from these incidents of the past and the signs that point toward the future that all is well if we keep our "Covenant with God"

Some of the examples of these impossibilities that have changed the course of history are:

The election of Abraham Lincoln in 1860 is our first example. Impossible! Yet it really happened. There could have been no intelligent prediction of the election outcome before it happened. Amazingly this came after the great debate on slavery in 1858. One would think that it would be impossible for Lincoln to be elected to any national office, especially as President, forget it! Stephen A. Douglas had defeated him for the office of Senator from Illinois after the Lincoln-Douglas debates on "Slavery". He seemed to have doomed his chances to ever be elected to any national office by making what appeared to be fatal blunders in his "House Divided Speech". When he quoted Jesus saying, "A House Divided Against Itself Can Not Stand", and then equated this with the slave question by adding to Jesus' statement "We must be all Slaves or All Free". This was like throwing gasoline to put out a fire. The Society was moving towards slavery as a fixed entity. The Supreme Court had given its "Dread Scott Decision",

101

rendering that a slave had no rights under any circumstance in any State. The Congress had passed the "Fugitive Slave Law", which stated that a slave may be picked up in any state and returned to his master regardless of the laws of that state!

In addition, "The Compromise of 1850" opened the way for slavery to come into the new formation of the western states that desired to join the "United States" according to the votes of each of those states. The "South's" strategy was to flood the new states with southern inhabitants in order to out vote the other residents of those states. The unexpected and that which was thought to be impossible happened in 1860. Only two years after the Lincoln-Douglas debate in 1858, Abraham Lincoln was elected to the office of President of the United States of America. More than this, he became the President who would lead the nation, to be a nation that would out-law chattel slavery and set a course that put in motion the demise of slavery throughout the world. The "Divided House" was brought together and we can declare legally "One National Under God with Liberty and Justice for all".

In his second inaugural address, Mr. Lincoln said this was an action which he believed that God was the Chief Director!

The second impossible happening, of which we can look at, is the defeat of the greatest powers of the world by the leadership of one little man.

The "Colonial System" was backed by the greatest consecration of powers of a few nations dominating the world. It was awesome for the nations of European domination that were entering this "Modern Age".

Great Britain was the leader of the Imperial System of Europe that controlled most of the globe. Great Britain often boasted that "The Sun Never Sets on the British Empire". Other nations such as France and Germany shared similar outlooks.

A few settlers could go into a country to follow an army, which had gone to make a way for them. Then a Country would become a colony of the "Mother" European Country. The age of modern "Fire Power" would make this happen rather quickly. Europe had the "fire power" and the adventurous men to back it up.

Yet there was one little man who did not possess the modern "fire power", nor did he have an army. This man brought the whole system to start breaking down. Impossible? Yet it happened!

The late Sir Winston Churchill, whose skillful leadership and a tremendous positive voice, had stated that he did not become the Kings/Queens First Minister to liquidate the Empire. Stating this, he had not considered the spiritual power of a little man who dressed in loincloth "wrapped around" like a peasant or an "untouchable". This little man, known as Gandhi was the one to bring about the impossible.

The imperialist said "Some day, but not now"!

Gandhi said "Now"! The Impossible?

Sir Winston Churchill initiated the start of the fall of the imperialistic system by negations with this little man who wore peasants clothes and had the 5th, 6th and 7th chapter of the book of Matthew read in his ashram each morning. Gandhi led the way in ending the greatest imperialistic system that the world has ever known.

The depression came and President Roosevelt made great strides in economic reforms, which in their aggregate forms effected the status of the Black people greatly. Yet, African American persons were still left adrift in a racial sea of haunting sharks. Their voting rights had been taken. This was their basic right to participate in the society's democratic process, which would give them true freedom to protect their rights as citizens.

The absence of the "right to vote" further negated the plight of African American people in America by rendering them as "second class citizens" if citizens at all. This factor also blunted economic leverage very much as the elected officials of the City, County and State performed their perspective duties with a total lack of allegiance to them.

Then there came along a man named King who led the people of color, the poor and indeed the whole nation to respond mostly positively and the impossible became a reality. This bold movement gave hope beyond expectations. Change became evident in the whole society. Hope came alive – Progress seemed more assured.

Following this, there came real setbacks. The birth of cults such as the Black Nationalist and the far right White groups some called the "Christian Right".

Then during the Nixon Administration, the white racists part of the Democratic Party's 'southern wing', left the Democratic Party and switched to the Republican Party carrying with them their baggage of racism.

This move seemed to have doomed the South and the nation's progressive movement. The same individuals now in charge, had been the crosses on which the civil liberties of Blacks had heretofore been crucified, seemed to be back in power.

This would cause the "Right Wing" of the country to appear as though they were "Carrying the Day" along with this.

Additionally, some of the Black leaders in a few of the "Progressive Movements" began to ask the government to carry them back to the "Old Separations Days" by granting them separate dormitories in colleges, and in some cases separate schools. In addition the request to support the school voucher movement, which is always a basic way to get around school integration, especially within the public schools now had new support! Other black groups began to show up like the "New Israelites", a Black race baiting group. Then others who cry to take us back to separate schools saying, "They were better for us" and "integration makes us worse off than we were before".

More than this we had the brake up of SNICK, in which so many Blacks and Whites had suffered together. C.O.R.E. quit singing, "We shall not be moved". These forgetting the pain and blood shed that both Blacks and

Whites had endured to bring us to the place where we were free to decent.

Then the Churches of the racially mixed and ethnic denominations began to organize Black groups that did not allow Whites to join. Others began to expand the false history that Martin Luther King had moved towards the position of Malcolm X. Some still asked was all this the work of **Dubois**, James Weldon Johnson and the martyrs along the way, including King, in Vain?

Sometimes it seemed as if the country was slipping back into the Pre "King" Pre "Civil Rights" thrust and some times back into the Pre Roosevelt day. The great work philosophy of the Debois, Walter White, James Weldon Johnson and hundreds of others and ever the great thrust of the church, from the pulpits both white and black, the great hymns for freedom gone. Some of these in the church gave way to the "hand clapping" so called gospel singing. These things of great spiritual values of the past now gave way to the individualistic gratification and the entertainment life selling of the gospel. In some of our cities when busloads of whites were going to so-called "Black Churches" to get their "Kicks" and cheap entertainment. This while one fourth or 25% of our nations Black Males were incarcerated in prisons, on parole or on probation and many of whom were innocent of any crime.

Also many young Black and Latino men found it unsafe to venture out in fear that they would be "stopped and searched" by police or other officers of the authoritarian "Law". There were more of these young men in jail than in College. While the church, that institution which had been in the marches and crusaders for liberty was too busy with their own affairs to cry to a society or to the States, "Thus Saith the Lord, this Oppression of My People Must Stop"!

In a time when the political Community had been lost in the craze for cutting taxes and when the "Contract With America" seemed to be a contract to oppress the poor and our "Striving seem to be losing".

When the only solution seemed to be political, one that would call the church back to its place to leading the society to a moral and ethical solution to problems backed up with a "Covenant With God"-There came a man from a little town in Arkansas names "Hope". He had risen to be the Governor of that State and also the President of the United States of America. Never! It could be said, "He is lose with women as David in the Bible was. His association is with the common people, especially Blacks was seen over and over again. But the man was elected!

At first he put forth some moderate politically safe policies for the country at work. Then he came out with his appointment system to make his cabinet and other executive appointments stating that the "Executive Department of Government should reflect the population of America". Then he did...He then went forward to put this in place. His words became his actions.

His cabinet looked like the United States of America, white, black, brown, and yellow (and if there was another color he included it). But all able people, not just tokens.

Many asked deep down, "Can this be"?

And others pledged deep down, "It Must Not Be"!

From the time of his elections, there were those who still said this must not be. How can we correct it? They had a serious problem.

The President's appointed people performed well. The country began to be economically stabilized.

There began to be a minute scrutinizing of the people appointed especially those who were of color or of ethnic minority background, and some women.

The Department of Agriculture, the Surgeon General, and The Department of Commerce became the frontline targets of those with hidden agendas.

The Hispanics and Blacks began taking the most direct scrutiny as the "Eyes of the World were focused o them, more than any appointed cabinet was ever seen.

Then, the head of the Department of Commerce was killed.

What about the Department of Agriculture, "Well he accepted two football tickets from a person with whom the Department was doing business".

"His close friend received a scholarship from one who was doing business". Which was returned.

The prosecutors proceeded to attack his Appointees as well as the President himself.

But alas, after years of interrogation the Secretary of The Department of Agriculture was declared innocent of "any" wrongdoing.

Did he receive an Apology? Of course not!

What about the Surgeon General?

Well we made it here "we got her out"

Well, she said "Auturism" in sex was better than pregnancy or getting Aids.

In fact we did not care what she said. We were getting at Him.

Out of this we will show that he made a bad appointment.

"What about the damage done to her"?

"You just don't get the point".

The problem with the cabinet fizzled out. What next?

What about the wife?

She is a lawyer. She is a lawyer who had practiced in Arkansas. Let us see what we can find on her. We must fine something to how on <u>Him</u>.

No nothing on his wife!

Well we must find something on Him!
Well you know he likes women.

Well who doesn't? "Ask Jerry Farwell that".

"We tried another woman situation when he was running for president but it seemed to make no difference".

Then a woman was found. It was a strange "Coincidence" that one interviewed woman who was told sordid details of her tryst with him and the listener, she recorded all was told to her.

And it "just happened" that the women who had the tapes was able to get them to the Chief Investigator who had been investigating on other rumors and alleged wrong doings. And after spending about forty million dollars, investigating "White River" – nothing!

The death at the White House, - nothing.

Election Campaign, - nothing.

Anything else,- nothing.

Then pay dirt – before the Mid-term elections – what coincidental timing. That fine American Woman who got this tape when all else had failed!

The investigation before the elections – What an opportunity!

The election could be the key. The Speaker of the House made great optimistic predictions about the gains, which his side waved as many as twenty seats would be gained.

With the Administration in the White House having such a scandal, he was thinking that he could not miss. All the bold appointments with the new thrust of inclusion were subject to go down the drain. If this happened it would be a long time before another President would attempt to have a Cabinet and the Executive Branches of America looking like the true face of America.

The days of the divided South would come again. The Crossing over could appoint tokens like Clarence Thomas, who would "go with the flow"!

The courts had given a victory in the voting potential of the Black People in the South. The districts would go back to having the districts that had been revamped to have a majority of white persons. Some of the districts in the southeast, this was done. This would take things back to where they we "used to be" and are supposed to be according to the Far Right.

The election came.

Those who believed in the inclusive government were overjoyed. The impossible had happened! All of the Black persons in the house were returned. More than this, there were strategic gains in the house for the democrats.

William M. James

This was the first time in more than one hundred years that the political party in the White House had gained in an off year election.

More over, the Senate remained the same in numbers with no gains or losses Subsequently, there were the state elections. Alabama, Georgia and the largest State of all California had all elected Governors and State houses as democrats.

Then, North Carolina's Republican Senator lost.

The overly zealous rejoicing of the Far Right turned to a grave situation.

The American electorate had spoken. They seemed to be saying "Stop, we have had enough of your investigations shutting down the government when we are prospering economically under this administration."

But the "Far Right" of the party seemed to press on with charges.

The Independent Council was urged to press forward!

The Speaker of the House was ousted, as if he was the cause of the Far Right's defeat.

Charges were pressed. Then they finally commanded the house to vote on charges of impeachment.

The strongest charge was that he "lied under oath".

They could not keep on the tract of accusing him of the Act of Adultery, because it was brought out that the new Speaker of the House was in the "Same Boat" and behold the head of the Judicial Committee conducting the prosecution was found to have dirty laundry.

But the prosecutors said "That maybe true, but they never lied under oath".

No one ever asked them or reminded them that these people were not asked about their acts under oath because they had never been requested to do so.

Both parties have practiced lying under oath for a very long time.

Most Senators, Representatives, Governors and Presidents have lied under oath for years! When they were asked, "Will you uphold the Constitution of the United States"? They put their hands up and swore that they would. A quick "Yes", and what follows? The Fourteenth Amendment of the Constitution demands "Equal treatment under law in all states".

This was not (and in some ways is still not) enforced in many States, where Black people are concerned.

The Black people were not allowed to vote, serve on jury duty, have schools supported by the states and experienced (and still do)many other deficiencies.

Therefore lying under oath was (and is) common practice of many public officials. There are hundreds, yes even thousands of Blacks that live under this system.

I am a witness.

When many of us had to leave home, we left the towns and counties where we were reared to go to high school.

The high schools for "Whites Only" were paid for by tax payers money, whereas no funding was allocated for Black Schools.

I know for I am one of those who saw white boys and girls bussed across the county where I grew up to a fine high school.

And when I finished grade school, a one room school built by the community (built by blacks out of their own resources) and sometimes located in the Methodist Episcopal Church there was <u>no</u> <u>High School</u> in the county for blacks!

The hope for our nation seems to be coming from the South.

What seemed impossible a few years ago now seems to be happening.

In spite of the past struggles, the hope for a Unified Nation with "Liberty and Justice for All" seems to be coming from unexpected places.

Many persons, who take public office, seem to be in line with the "Covenant With God". The Presidents who have boldly sought to bring our great nation to see what "Equality Under God" is, have southern origins.

The Presidents whom were most progressive, and proactive were Lyndon Johnson, Jimmy Carter and William Clinton.

The president who integrated the Army was Harry Truman.

There have been some outstanding Senators such as Claud Pepper of Florida, Graham of North Carolina, Senators Albert Gore Senior and Albert Gore Junior of Tennessee and The Honorable Huge Black of Alabama as Supreme Court Judge.

The Honorable Senator Hollins of South Carolina that received an over whelming vote from African American voters from that State.

We also had Chief Justice Vincent from Kentucky who ignited the turning point of the Supreme Courts over turning of the "Separate But Equal rules".

These and others have given us a "Ray of Hope for the Future"!

William M. James

About the Author

The Reverend Dr. William James was born in Meadville, Mississippi. He attended high school at Monroe Louisana (there were no high schools for black people in Franklin County Mississippi at this time, where Meadville is located.) After high school he went to Southern Christian Institute, Mt. Buleah College at Edwards, Mississippi where he received an A.A degree. He went from there to Butler University at Indiana where he received a B.S. degree (School of Liberal Arts) and a B.S.L. from Butler School of Religion. From there he went to Drew University in Madison, New Jersey there he received a B.D. (now M. Div.) and also received a M.A. in religion. Drew awarded him a Doctor of Humane Letters. He has taken special courses at Chicago University and the Jewish Theological Seminary in New York.

Doctor James served as Pastor of the United Methodist Church in New York, East Calvery, where he helped to promote early childhood education. This he did his first civic work as he served on the late Mayor LaGuardia's Commission on "War Time Care of Children". He served at Trinity United Methodist Church in the Bronx and brought the church from zero members to 900 members in the eight years of his pastorate. There he worked with street gangs and began to be called a "Street Minister". After Trinity Church he became Senior Minister at the Metropolitan United Methodist Church which he led for some 33 years. When he left Metropolitan he became the Executive Director of the Multi Ethnic Center located at Drew and working with Boston University School of Religion and Wesley Theological Seminary in Washington,

D.C. He taught "Dynamics of Urban Ministry" at Drew University for ten years. He now serves as Executive Director of the Ministerial Interfaith Association of New York. Dr. James has been a part of many organizations in the United Methodist Church and in the City of New York He has sent some 3600 young people through college; 72 of these became clergy persons of various denominations.